THE HARMONY OF HEARTS

CELTIC REFLECTIONS ON THE GOSPELS

CHRIS MCAULEY

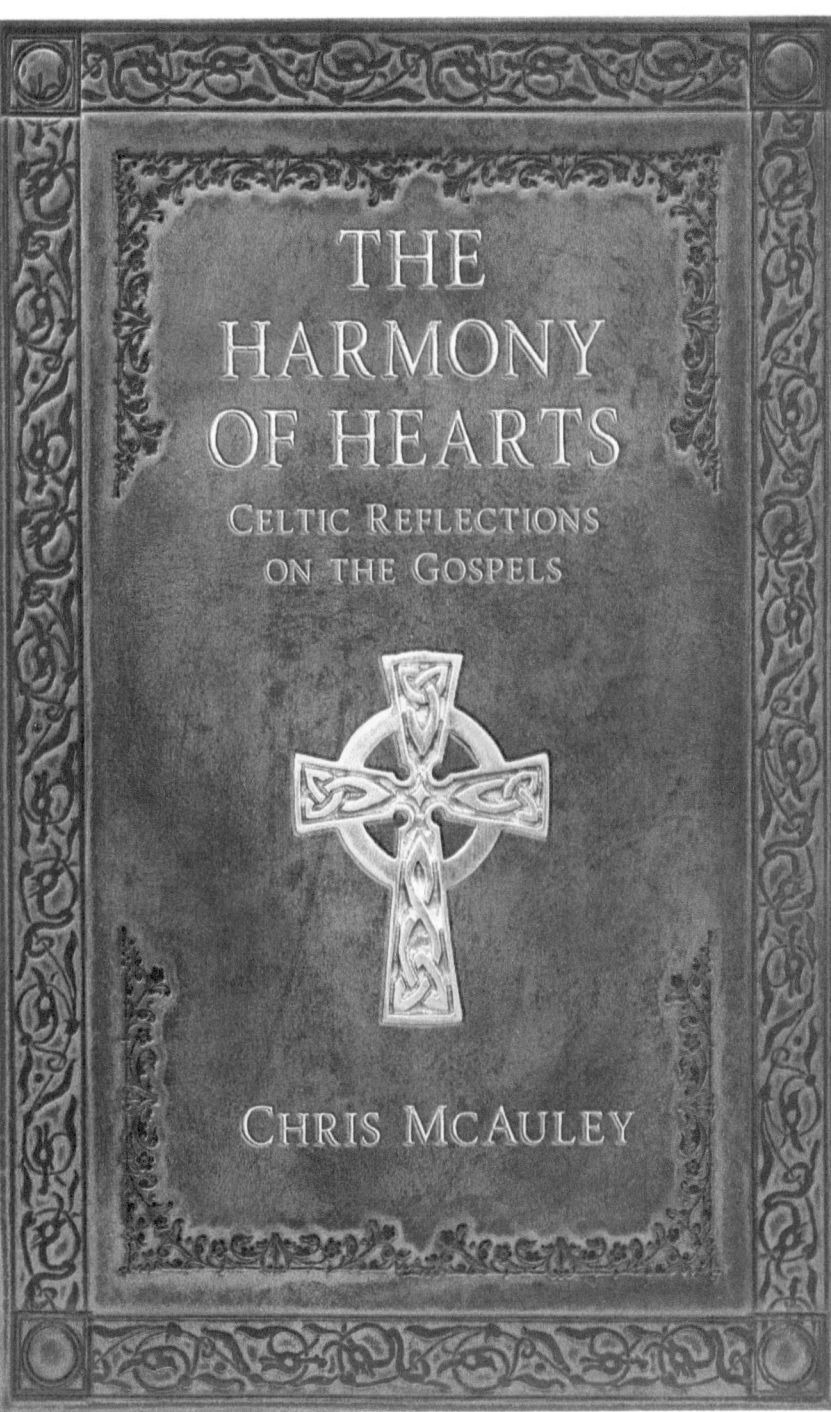

Published by Watertower Hill Publishing
Tulsa, OK
Joshua Daughrity - Publisher
www.watertowerhill.com
Copyright © 2025 by Chris McAuley. All rights reserved.

Cover wrap by Susan Roddey
at The Snark Shop by Pheonix and Fae Creations.
Cover design and internal format/editing by Joshua Loyd Fox and Heather Daughrity at Watertower Hill Publishing.
Copyright © 2025 Watertower Hill Publishing. All rights reserved.

No part of this book may be reproduced in any form without prior written permission of the author and publisher—other than for "fair use" as brief quotations embodied in articles and reviews.

Author's Note

All character and names in this book are biblical, and canonical. No name, nor descriptive of any named person, living or deceased is otherwise implied. Any similarities to other people, living or deceased, is purely by coincidence. Author and Publisher are not liable for any likeness described herein.

Library of Congress Control Number: 2025936353

Hardback ISBN: 978-1-965546-13-0
eBook ASIN: B0F4G87661

Printed in the United States of America
10 9 8 7 6 5 4 3 2 1

To my Parents.

And my publishers at Watertower Hill.

Contents

Introduction: A Journey of Discovery 13
Revealing the Christ: An Exploration of the Gospel Narratives 15
Chapter 1: Echoes of Creation 3
- The Birth of Light — *Genesis 1-4* 5
- Celestial Echoes – *Luke 1:5-25* 7
- Whispers of Incarnation – *Luke 1:26-38* 9
- Echoes of Joy – *Luke 1:39-45* 11
- A Song of Grace – *Luke 1:46* 13
- A Prophetic Dawn – *Luke 1:57-80* 15
- Emmanuel's Promise – *Matt 1:18-25* 17
- Starlit Miracle – *Matt. 1:24-25 / Luke 2:1-7* 19
- The Shepherds' Song – *Luke 2:8-14* 21
- Echoes of Wonder – *Luke 2:15-20* 23
- Simeon's Vision – *Luke 2:22-38* 25
- Guided by Stars – *Matthew 2:1-12* 27
- Refuge in the Shadows – *Matt. 2:13-18* 29
- Return from Exile – *Matt. 2:19-23/Luke 2:39* 31
- Growing in Grace – *Luke 2:40-52* 32
- Wisdom's Temple – *Luke 2:41-50* 34
- The Carpenter's Son – *Luke 2:51-52* 36

Chapter 2: The Voice of the Wilderness 37
- An Outcrying Voice – *Mark 1:1-4* 39
- Igniting the Soul – *Mark 1:2-8* 41
- A Refining Fire – *Matthew 3:11-12* 43
- The Prophet's Voice – *Matthew 14:4-12* 45

Chapter 3: The Dawn of Transformation 47
- The Lamb of God – *John 1:29-34* 49
- Temptation and Triumph – *Matthew 4:1-11* 51
- Invitation and Revelation – *John 1:35-51* 53
- The Miracle of Transformation — *John 2:1-11* 55
- The Cleansing of the Temple – *John 2:12-22* 56
- The Knowing Hearts – *John 2:23-25* 57
- Born Anew – *John 3:1-21* 58
- Rivers of Faith – *John 3:22-36* 59
- Samaritan Encounter – *John 4:1-4* 60

Thirst Quenched – *John 4:5-42* 61
Returning Faith – *John 4:43-45* 63
Chapter 4: Radiant Lights in the North 65
Faith's Healing Touch – *John 4:46-54* 67
Proclamation and Rejection – *Luke 4:16-30* 68
The Seeds of Truth – *Mark 4:13-20* 70
Casting Nets of Faith – *Matthew 4:18-22* 72
Authority Unveiled – *Luke 4:31-37* 73
Healing Touch – *Mark 1:29-34* 74
A Healing Light – *Matthew 4:23-25* 75
An Unclean Cry – *Mark 1:40-45* 76
Faith's Unveiling – *Luke 5:17-26* 78
The Call of Transformation – *Matthew 9:9-13* 80
New Wine, New Wineskins – *Mark 2:18-22* 81
The Withered is Restored – *Luke 6:6-11* 83
Hope for the Broken – *Matthew 12:15-21* 84
Chosen Disciples – *Luke 6:12-16* 85
Sermon on the Mount – *Matt. 5:1-Matt.7:29* 87
Faith that Moves Mountains – *Luke 7:1-10* 89
Restoration Beyond Tears – *Luke 7:11-17* 91
Confirming Hope – *Matthew 11:2-9* 92
Invitation to Rest – *Matthew 11:20-30* 93
A Sinner's Redemption – *Luke 7:36-50* 95
Divided Hearts – *Mark 3:20-30* 96
Seeking Signs – *Matthew 12:38-45* 97
Family in Faith – *Mark 3:31-35* 98
Master of the Storm – *Mark 4:35-41* 99
Liberation of the Tormented – *Luke 8:26-39* 100
The Resurrected Life — *Mark 5:21-43* 102
Eyes of Faith – *Matthew 9:27-31* 104
Words of Wonder – *Matthew 9:32-34* 105
The Veil of Familiarity – *Matthew 13:53-58* 106
The Journey of Empowerment – *Luke 9:1-6* 107
A Tragic Tale of Conscience – *Mark 6:14-29* 108
A Feast of Abundance – *John 6:1-14* 109
Walking on Water – *John 6:15-21* 110
The Gentle Touch – *Mark 6:53-56* 112
The Matters of the Heart – *Matthew 15:1-20* 114

The Bread of Abundance – *Mark 8:1-9* 116
Seeking Signs – *Mark 8:10-13* 118
Yeast of the Pharisees – *Matthew 16:5-12* 119
The Test of Allegiance – *John 6:67-71* 120
The Cost of Discipleship – *Luke 9:22-25* 121
Transfiguration's Glimpse – *Mark 9:1* 122
The Veil of Understanding — *Luke 9:43-45* 123
The Coin of Divine Provision – *Matt. 17:24-27* 124
Lessons in Humility & Salt – *Mark 9:33-50* 125
Divine Timing – *John 7:2-9* 126
Seeking Wisdom – *Matthew 19:1* 127
Chapter 5: The Celestial Journey 129
Whispers of Faith and Doubt – *John 7:2-53* 131
Mercy's Embrace – *John 8:1-11* 133
Light of the World – *John 8:12-20* 135
Freedom's Call – *John 8:21-59* 136
The Light of Sight – *John 9:1-41* 138
The Shepherd's Call – *John 10:1-21* 140
Sent as Laborers – *Luke 10:1-24* 142
The Good Samaritan – *Luke 10:25-37* 144
The Choice of Mary & Martha – *Luke 10:38-42* 146
Teach Us to Pray – *Luke 11:1-13* 148
The Light & Darkness – *Luke 11:14-36* 150
White Sepulchers – *Luke 11:37-54* 152
Fear Not, Little Flock – *Luke 12:1-59* 154
Reflection on Tragedy – *Luke 13:1-5* 156
The Parable of the Fig Tree – *Luke 13:6-9* 157
Healed on a Sabbath – *Luke 13:10-17* 158
The Seed & the Leaven – *Luke 13:18-21* 160
Returning to the Source – *John 10:40-42* 161
The Great Banquet's Call – *Luke 14:1-24* 162
The Price of Faith – *Luke 14:25-35* 163
Parables of Lost and Found – *Luke 15:1-32* 164
of Stewardship & Riches – *Luke 16:1-31* 165
Faith, Forgiveness, & Service – *Luke 17:1-10* 166
Restored from the Dead – *John 11:1-44* 167
Seeds of Decision – *John 11:45-54* 168
Healing at the Fringe – *Luke 17:11* 169

Kingdom's Mystery Unveiled – *Luke 17:20-37* 170
of Humility & Persistence – *Luke 18:1-14* 172
Children & the Kingdom – *Matt. 19:13-15* 174
The Rich Ruler's Dilemma – *Mark 10:17-31* 175
The Generous Vineyard Owner – *Matt. 20:1-16* 177
The Foretelling of Suffering – *Luke 18:31-34* 179
The Servant's Call – *Matthew 20:20-28* 180
Blind Bartimaeus – *Luke 18:35-43* 181
Zacchaeus' Redemption – *Luke 19:1-10* 183
The Faithful Steward – *Luke 19:11-27* 185
The Alabaster Offering – *John 11:55-John 12:1* 187
Witness of Lazarus – *John 12:9-11* 189
Chapter 6: Crowned in Sacrifice, Resurrected in Glory 191
Triumphal Entry – *John 12:12-19* 193
The Cleansing of the Temple – *Matt. 21:10-19* 194
The Hour of Glory – *John 12:20-50* 195
Authority & Parables – *Mark 11:27-Mark 12:12* 196
Cunning Questions – *Luke 20:20-26* 197
Resurrection's Light – *Mark 12:18-27* 198
Love's Command – *Matthew 22:34-40* 199
Lord and Descendant – *Luke 20:41-44* 200
Beware the Hypocrisy – *Mark 12:38-40* 201
The Widow's Offering – *Mark 12:41-44* 202
Signs of the Times – *Luke 21:5-36* 203
The Parable of Preparedness – *Matt. 25:1-46* 204
The Anointing of Jesus – *Mark 14:1-2* 205
A Fragrant Offering – *Matthew 26:6-13* 206
Betrayal's Whispers – *Luke 22:3-6* 207
Preparation's Prelude – *Luke 22:7-13* 208
Communion's Covenant – *Mark 14:17* 209
Servant's Love – *John 13:1-20* 210
Shadows of Betrayal – *Matthew 26:21-25* 211
The Weight of Denial – *John 13:31-38* 212
The Cup of the New Covenant – *Luke 22:17-20* 213
A Promise of Comfort – *John 14:1- John 17:26* 214
Gethsemane's Agony – *Matthew 26:30-46* 216
Betrayed with a Kiss – *Matthew 26:47-56* 218
The High Priests Inquiry – *John 18:2* 220

In the Courtyard's Chill – *John 18:12-23* 222
The Mocking Trial – *Matthew 26:57-68* 224
Denial and Redemption – *Matthew 26:58-75* 226
The Verdict of Truth – *Luke 22:66-71* 227
The Weight of Regret – *Matthew 27:3-10* 228
Before the Judgement Seat – *Luke 23:1-7* 229
Herod's Curiosity – *Luke 23:6-12* 230
Mockery and Scorn – *Matthew 27:27-30* 231
The Journey to Calvary – *John 19:16-17* 232
A Mother's Sorrow – *John 19:18-27* 233
Darkness and Victory – *Matthew 27:45-50* 234
The Veil of Mystery – *Luke 23:45-49* 235
The Silent Tomb – *Mark 15:42-46* 236
The Empty Tomb – *Luke 24:1-11* 237
Dawn of Resurrection – *John 20:1-10* 238
Risen Hope – *John 20:11-18* 240
The Web of Deceit – *Matthew 28:11-15* 242
The Road to Emmaus – *Luke 24:13-35* 243
Thomas Believes – *John 20:26-31* 245
A Miraculous Catch – *John 21:1-25* 247
The Great Commission – *Matthew 28:16-20* 249
Ascension's Blessing – *Luke 24:50-53* 251
Appendix 255

Introduction: A Journey of Discovery

In a world filled with turmoil, where echoes of violence and the shadows of betrayal seem to permeate every corner of our lives, I found myself seeking solace in the timeless wisdom of the Gospels. Delving into the pages of Matthew, Mark, Luke, and John, I discovered a refuge of truth and grace that held the power to not only transform my perspective, but bring some light into the darkness of the world which surrounded me.

I had grown up with the stories contained within the Gospels; they were a familiar companion on my spiritual journey. They offered guidance and inspiration as I navigated the twists and turns of life. Yet, as the noise of the modern world began to distract me, I found myself distancing from those sacred texts. The very essence of their teachings, so powerful and profound, seemed overshadowed by the chaos that surrounded me.

It wasn't that I had abandoned my faith or lost belief in the message of Christ's love. Rather I had inadvertently allowed the noise of the world to momentarily obscure the depth of that love. It was as if I had closed my eyes to the radiance of a sunrise, unable to fully appreciate its beauty amidst the shadows.

During my other work as a horror and science fiction writer I felt a call to return to the Gospels. To rediscover the timeless truths that had, for centuries, held the power to heal, unite, and uplift. It was a call to unearth the treasures of wisdom that could illuminate a path forward—a path paved with love, compassion, and the unwavering promise of grace.

In the pages that follow, I invite you to join me on this journey of rediscovery. Together we will explore the profound messages of the

Gospels and weave them with the tapestry of Celtic Spirituality. This is the language of my people and connects us deeply to the earth, to each other, and to the divine presence that surrounds us. Let us look for the ties which bind us together, even in the face of adversity, and weave them into a narrative that celebrates God's boundless love for all beings.

May these reflections and poems serve as a lantern amidst the shadows, guiding us toward the heart of a love that transcends the darkness which can cloud our minds and hurt our souls. As we embark on this spiritual pilgrimage, may we find solace, inspiration, and renewal in the timeless truths that have power to heal a fractured world.

Pax,
Chris McAuley

Revealing the Christ: An Exploration of the Gospel Narratives

The Gospels are the foundational narratives of the New Testament. They offer us an intimate and multi-faceted portrait of Jesus Christ, the central figure of Christianity. Written by different authors from diverse perspectives, the Gospels present a comprehensive account of Jesus' life, teachings, miracles, crucifixion, and resurrection. As we embark on our poetic journey through these books, let us examine each of the Gospels and uncover how they portray the rich tapestry of experiences that defined the ministry of Jesus.

In the pages of Matthew, we encounter Jesus as the long-awaited Messiah, bridging the Old and New Testaments. Matthew's Gospel emphasizes the fulfillment of prophecies, the teachings of Jesus through parables, and His role as the embodiment of the divine covenant. Each story unfolds with a clear intention to reveal Jesus as the rightful King, offering spiritual insight and guidance to His followers.

Mark's Gospel, known for its brevity and vivid descriptions, emphasizes the power and authority of Jesus. Through its action-packed narrative, Mark paints Jesus as a dynamic healer and miracle-worker, while also highlighting the personal struggles of His disciples. In Mark's account, we find the essence of a servant King, who embodies selflessness and dedication to His mission.

Luke's Gospel unveils Jesus as the compassionate Savior who reaches out to the marginalized and brings hope to the downtrodden.

With detailed accounts of Jesus' parables, teachings, and His interactions with women and the outcasts of society, Luke's narrative highlights the universality of Christ's message of redemption and the profound impact it has on every soul.

Lastly, the Gospel of John stands out as a theological masterpiece, delving deep into the divinity of Christ. Through poetic language and profound discourses, John's Gospel invites us to contemplate Jesus as the Word made flesh, the light of the world, and the source of eternal life. His account invites us to explore the mysteries of Christ's identity and His transformative role in the lives of believers.

As we journey through these Gospel accounts, we are invited to immerse ourselves in the life, teachings, and ministry of Jesus Christ. Each Gospel paints a distinct perspective, offering us a more holistic view of this remarkable figure who continues to impact humanity to this day. From His humble birth to His triumphant resurrection, the Gospels guide us through a transformative exploration of faith, love, and redemption. Join us as we traverse these sacred narratives, seeking to understand the essence of Jesus' eternal mission and its relevance to our lives today.

Chapter 1: Echoes of Creation

In the sacred tapestry of human history, there are moments which transcend time, bridging the gap between the ancient past and the unfolding future. At the heart of this tapestry lies the birth of Christ, an event that not only marks the beginning of a new era but also echoes with the resonance of creation itself.

As we journey through the pages of the Gospels, we are not merely recounting a historical narrative; we are immersing ourselves in a profound symphony of spirituality, woven with threads of divinity, prophecy, and human experience. It is a story that connects the ancient echoes of Genesis—the dawn of creation—with the radiant promises of Christ's birth—the dawn of redemption.

In these poems, we explore the intricate interplay between the birth of Jesus Christ and the creation of the world as told in the Book of Genesis. We delve into the deep connections that link these two pivotal narratives, each informing and enriching the other. Just as God's divine breath brought forth the universe in Genesis, so too does the birth of Christ herald a new creation—a transformation of hearts and souls.

We journey alongside Mary and Joseph, shepherds, and Magi, as they experience wonder, doubt, faith, and adoration. Through their eyes, we witness the divine unfolding amidst the ordinary, the sacred mingling with the mundane. These poems capture the intimate moments, the whispered conversations, the dreams and prophecies that bridge the gap between the divine and the human, between Genesis and the Gospels.

As we reflect on the birth of Christ, we invite you to journey with us in a meditative exploration between creation, incarnation, and redemption. May these verses illuminate the timeless significance of Christ's birth, revealing how it intertwines with the very fabric of existence, resonating through the ages and guiding us toward a deeper understanding of the mysteries that bind us to God's eternal plan.

The Birth of Light — *Genesis 1-4*

In the beginning, a canvas blank,
A universe unformed, a cosmic span,
God's breath swept over the void's expanse,
A symphony of creation, a divine dance.

With whispers of light, the darkness fled,
Stars ignited like dreams overhead,
Galaxies spun like silken thread,
Infinite cosmos, a tapestry spread.

Upon the waters, a gentle touch,
Life's cradle formed, a world to clutch,
Mountains arose, majestic and bold,
As oceans and rivers their stories told.

The came the creatures, diverse and rare,
Wings of flight and creatures that dare,
Forests and jungles, deserts so wide,
In each corner of Earth, life did abide.

But a masterpiece awaited, a crown unfurled,
In the image of God, humankind swirled,
From dust and clay, a form took shape,
A reflection divine, a spirit to drape.

With Love's tender breath, a soul enkindled,
In Eden's embrace, innocence mingled,
Yet choice brought a twist, a tale of desire,
Knowledge and consequence intertwined like fire.

In Genesis' pages, a tale unfolds,
Of creation's beauty and stories untold,
God's hand in the making, a world so vast,
A symphony of wonders, a future cast.

From the beginning, a spark ignited,
A universe of love, brilliantly sighted,
And still, through the ages, that love does flow,
In every heartbeat, in every soul's glow.

Meditation: Reflect on the spark of love which ignited the universe, a brilliance that still courses through the ages. Imagine this love flowing through every heartbeat, every soul's glow—a reminder that we are part of a cosmic dance, forever connected to the Divine, and forever echoing the birth of light.

Celestial Echoes – *Luke 1:5-25*

In the hush of sacred chambers, I knelt and prayed,
A lifetime of longing in each whispered word conveyed,
My voice, a vessel of hope, reaching the divine,
Begging for a miracle, a gift to call mine.

My days had aged, my hair turned silver and gray,
Barren were the years, no child came to stay,
But within the temple's holy space, an angel appeared,
With tidings of joy, erasing doubts and fears.

"A son," he declared, his voice like music's grace,
My disbelief shifted, a smile on my weathered face,
Yet my voice faltered, a question filled the air,
How could this be, a child so rare?

Dumbstruck I stood, a silent messenger's decree,
For doubting the angel's words, a price to be paid by me,
A hush enveloped my soul, my voice was stolen away,
A silence profound, until that promised day.

Months rolled on, within my heart a growing flame,
My Elizabeth, her joy an unspoken name,
A secret, a treasure, a life knit within,
A promise of redemption, a pardon for my sin.

Then came the moment, swift as a fleeting dream,
Within a room filled with moonlight's silver gleam,
Elizabeth's laughter, a melody of grace,
As the miracle unfolded, love's tender embrace.

With tiny fingers and eyes that glistened like dawn,
Our son was born and the veil of silence withdrawn,
In awe, I beheld him, this child of prophecy,
A messenger destined to set hearts and spirits free.

As my voice returned, I praised the divine,
For in this miracle's light, a purpose did shine,
John, we named him, a blessing from above,
A beacon of hope, a testament to God's love.

Oh, the joy that filled me, a cup overflowing,
In John's eyes, a promise, a destiny showing,
My heart's gratitude an echo in the night,
For from doubt to belief, I journeyed toward the light.

Meditation: Reflect on the journey of faith and transformation, from longing to fulfillment, from silence to praise. Consider the depth of devotion that led to this moment of celestial echoes, a reminder that even in our doubts, the divine's love can speak through the chambers of our hearts.

Whispers of Incarnation – *Luke 1:26-38*

In a humble abode, where prayers entwine,
Mary, a soul pure, a heart's gentle shrine,
An ordinary day, yet destined to unfold,
A tale of heaven's whisper, a story untold.

A presence unseen, a rustle of wings,
An angel's embrace, a message that sings,
"Greetings, favored one," the celestial voice,
A proclamation divine, a destiny's choice.

Startled yet steadfast, Mary's eyes met the light,
A messenger of God, dispelling the night,
Fear and wonder danced in a delicate blend,
As the angel's words whispered, a message to send.

"Behold, you will conceive, a miracle rare,
A son to be born, beyond earthly compare,
Jesus, His name, a Savior He'll be,
Emmanuel, God with us, for all to see."

A question arose, "How can this be so?
I know not a man, this truth you bestow."
The answer, a miracle, the Holy Spirit's grace,
A child of divinity, in Mary's embrace.

A surrender profound, her heart's gentle nod,
A journey to Bethlehem, ordained by God,
In Mary's "Let it be," humanity's course was swayed,
As heaven and earth converged, in love's serenade.

A mother she became, to the King of kings,
In her womb, eternity's story takes wing,
In her "yes" to the divine, a promise unfurls,
A tale of redemption, of God's love for the world.

So let us remember this moment so sweet,
When an angel's words made Mary's heart beat,
Announcing a birth, a hope's sacred mirth,
A promise fulfilled, in the miracle of Christ's birth.

Meditation: Reflect on the significance of this moment—the whispers of incarnation that resound through time. Picture Mary's heart beating in rhythm with the angel's message, a proclamation of hope and fulfillment.

Echoes of Joy – *Luke 1:39-45*

Two souls, kin in spirit though years apart,
Elizabeth and Mary, their destinies start,
A meeting ordained by the hands of time,
A moment where lives and purpose entwine.

In the heart of Judea, in a quiet abode,
Elizabeth's joy, a radiant ode,
Expectant she was, her belly a bloom,
A life within life, placed in a sacred room.

Mary arrived, a visitor's grace,
A journey to share, a smile on her face,
Two women united, a tale to unfold,
In the depths of their beings, stories untold.

As their voices intertwined, laughter and tears,
A symphony of connection, dispelling all fears,
Elizabeth's voice, a welcome embrace,
Mary's spirit soared in the home's gentle space.

Then in a moment, a miracle took hold,
As John leapt within, his spirit untold,
The unborn prophet, recognizing the way,
A leap of joy in the presence of that day.

Elizabeth's exclamation, a truth profound,
"Blessed are you among women," was the sound,
Mary, humbled and touched, in awe's embrace,
A bond formed in faith; two souls interlace.

In the heartbeats of life, in the depths of their gaze,
A sacred communion, as time's fabric sways,
The unborn herald and Savior to be,
A dance of destiny, beyond what eyes see.

In this embrace of wombs, a story so grand,
Two vessels of purpose, guided by God's hand,
A meeting of souls, a friendship's sweet start,
Elizabeth and Mary, bound by a sacred heart.

Meditation: Reflect on the beauty of this encounter—the echo of joy that resonates through time. Envision Elizabeth and Mary, two souls intertwined, bound by the twin fulfilled promises of God and the unique destinies that connect them.

A Song of Grace – Luke 1:46

In the stillness of twilight, a soul ablaze,
Mary's heart burst forth in a hymn of praise,
A melody woven from depths of her core,
A song of surrender, of faith evermore.

"My soul magnifies the Lord," she sang,
A chorus of gratitude, the heavens rang,
For in her womb, a miracle was found,
A Savior's birth, love unbound.

"Lowly handmaiden," she humbly spoke,
Chosen by God, her spirit awoke,
A vessel for grace, a conduit of light,
In her "yes," a world transformed from night.

Generations to come would call her blessed,
A mother of hope, in God's plan to invest,
Her song, a tapestry of justice and might,
A promise of redemption, a future so bright.

The proud scattered, the humble exalted,
A world turned on its axis, by love assaulted,
Mary's heart poured forth in words divine,
A declaration of God's design.

In her song, the hungry would be fed,
The humble lifted, hope spread,
A symphony of justice, a chorus of grace,
A divine dance in time and space.

From generation to generation, her voice reverberates,
A testament to faith, love that never abates,
In Mary's song, a legacy's bloom,
A tribute to a love that conquers gloom.

Meditation: Consider the legacy of Mary's voice—an echo of faith, a testament to a love that remains unwavering. Envision her song as a bloom that spans generations, a tribute to a love that conquers all darkness and heralds a new dawn.

A Prophetic Dawn – *Luke 1:57-80*

In the fullness of time, a miracle's embrace,
Elizabeth's womb, a vessel of grace,
John's birth arrived, a dawn breaking clear,
A promise fulfilled; a tale held dear.

Neighbors and kin, rejoicing with glee,
"The Lord has shown great mercy," they agree,
Naming the child, a question on lips,
"John?" they asked, doubting Elizabeth's quips.

Zechariah, still silenced by angel's decree,
Asked for a writing tablet, a gesture of plea,
Inscribed his name, confirming the choice,
And as his voice returned, his heart found its voice.

With a voice regained, Zechariah sang,
A song of prophecy, from the depths it sprang,
"Blessed be the Lord," his heart's jubilant cry,
A prophet's song, to the heavens it'd fly.

"A horn of salvation," he proclaimed with might,
"Redemption's dawn, a resplendent light,"
John, the prophet, a herald to be,
Preparing the way for the Savior to see.

A journey unfolding, the child grew strong,
In the wilderness, where faith and hope throng,
Guided by God's hand, in wisdom and grace,
Prepared for the task, his destined place.

From the silence of doubt to the proclamation bold,
A tale of transformation, a story of old,
In Luke's pages, this chapter unfolds,
A promise kept; in every tale it holds.

Meditation: Reflect on the intricate tapestry of events—a prophetic dawn breaking through the pages of scripture. Envision John's journey, a beacon of faith and hope, as his story intertwines with the broader narrative of God's plan.

Emmanuel's Promise – Matt 1:18-25

In Bethlehem's shadows, a love took root,
A story untold, a tale of pursuit,
Joseph and Mary, a bond pure and strong,
Yet a secret they held, a mystery's song.

Betrothed they were, a future envisioned,
Yet Mary's news their world imprisoned,
With child she was, a truth yet unspoken,
A divine conception, a promise awoken.

Joseph, a man of honor and grace,
Pondered the path, the love he'd embrace,
In dreams he found solace, an angel's voice,
Guiding his heart, revealing the choice.

"Fear not to take Mary as your wife,"
The angel proclaimed, a message to life,
A child of promise, a Savior divine,
A future unfolded, a tale intertwines.

In Joseph's dream, his doubts were dissolved,
A journey of faith, his heart now resolved,
He took Mary in, their destinies twined,
In love's tender grace, in faith enshrined.

Emmanuel, "God with us," they'd name,
In the Bethlehem stable, love's fire aflame,
Joseph's dream, a testament of belief,
A story of love that would conquer grief.

Meditation: Reflect on the profound promise embedded within this story—the promise of God's presence among us, the promise of a love which transcends understanding. Envision Joseph and Mary's journey, a journey that embodies the essence of faith and love setting the stage for the birth of Emmanuel.

STARLIT MIRACLE – MATT. 1:24-25 / LUKE 2:1-7

In Bethlehem's quiet, beneath a sky so vast,
A miracle unfolded, a story to forever last,
A stable's humble embrace, a manger's tender bed,
The Savior's birth, a tale that angels spread.

A star hung low, a radiant guide,
Guiding the way, a celestial stride,
Shepherds in fields, their hearts astir,
A chorus of angels, their song a whisper.

"Glory to God," their voices proclaimed,
"Peace on Earth," a message untamed,
A Savior born, a hope to impart,
A light to illuminate every heart.

In Mary's arms, a miracle divine,
God in human form, love's grand design,
Joseph, a guardian, his heart aglow,
As heaven and earth converged below.

Magi from afar, their gifts did bear,
Gold, frankincense, and myrrh to share,
Symbolizing homage, prophecy, and grace,
In their journey's end, love found its place.

In a stable's shelter, a sacred scene,
A mother's tender touch, a newborn's gleam,
A world forever changed, a promise born anew,
In the manger's embrace, hope's dawn grew.

The Christ child, a gift of love untold,
A beacon of light in a world grown cold,
In Bethlehem's stillness, in a starlit night,
The birth of hope, a wondrous sight.

Meditation: Consider the profound impact of this starlit miracle—the birth of a promise that would change the course of history. Envision the tender beauty of the manger scene, a moment that encapsulates the essence of love, hope, and the transformative power of Christ's arrival.

The Shepherds' Song – *Luke 2:8-14*

Beneath a star-strewn canvas, a shepherd's night,
Fields stretched wide, bathed in moonlight,
In quiet contemplation, their flocks they kept,
When suddenly, a realm of heavens swept.

An angel appeared, a figure of light,
A radiance dazzling, dispelling the night,
"Fear not," the angel's voice, gentle and kind,
A proclamation of joy to humble hearts aligned.

"I bring you tidings of great joy," he sang,
A Savior born, a heavenly clang,
In Bethlehem's town, a manger's embrace,
The Christ child's birth, a love's sweet grace.

A chorus of angels, a host on high,
Their voices joined, echoing through the sky,
"Glory to God," they sang, a celestial choir,
"Peace on Earth," their melody, higher and higher.

With hearts astir, the shepherds took flight,
Toward the manger's glow, in the still of night,
A journey of wonder, a moment divine,
To witness the miracle, the sacred sign.

In the stable's hush, they knelt in awe,
Before the newborn King, a love without flaw,
In that manger's embrace, hope came alive,
A promise fulfilled, as angels did strive.

Alleluias resounded, a melody pure,
A song of redemption, of love to endure,
In Luke's verses, this chapter unfolds,
Shepherds and angels, a tale to be told.

Meditation: Imagine the resounding alleluias that fill the air, a melody that springs forth from hearts brimming with pure devotion. Contemplate the redemptive power of this song, a song that will endure through the generations. Envision Luke's verses unfurling, a chapter of scripture that tells of shepherds and angels, a timeless tale of grace, love, and divine intervention.

ECHOES OF WONDER – *LUKE 2:15-20*

Upon Bethlehem's outskirts, a quiet night's veil,
Shepherds stood watch by moonlight pale,
A voice from the heavens broke stillness and dearth—
An angel proclaiming the Savior's birth.

With haste they journeyed, a path uncharted,
Their souls stirred, their doubts departed,
A stable's manger, a humble scene,
In wonder they stood, in awe serene.

The Christ child lay, a promise fulfilled,
Their hearts in stillness, their spirits stilled,
A chorus of angels, a prophecy bright,
A Savior's birth, a beacon of light.

In this sacred moment, they bore witness true,
The shepherds' eyes with wonder grew,
Their voices trembled, their joy overflowed,
A tale of God's love, forever bestowed.

From stable to village, the shepherds proclaimed,
The news of the Christ child, the Savior's name,
A marvel shared, a story of grace,
In their adoration, love found its place.

In Luke's verses, this chapter unwinds,
Shepherds and angels, their destinies twined,
A tale of wonder, a journey's embrace,
As shepherds beheld love's radiant face.

Meditation: Reflect on the essence of this chapter—an echo of wonder, a symphony of journey and revelation. Picture the shepherds as they stand in the presence of love's radiant face, their lives forever transformed by the miracle they have witnessed.

Simeon's Vision – *Luke 2:22-38*

In the temple's sacred halls, a moment divine,
A story of destiny, a purpose's sign,
Mary and Joseph, a child in their hold,
A Savior revealed, a future foretold.

Simeon, a just man, his heart's fervent plea,
Guided by Spirit, his eyes longed to see,
He cradled the infant, a promise unfurled,
In his arms rested hope for the world.

"Lord, let your servant depart in peace," he cried,
For his eyes had beheld, his doubts set aside,
The Light of revelation, in the child's gaze,
A Redeemer's presence, a love that stays.

Anna, a prophetess, her years spent in prayer,
In the temple's embrace, she dwelt in God's care,
Her heart filled with gratitude, her spirit alight,
As she witnessed the child, her faith taking flight.

Together, Simeon and Anna, souls wise and true,
Their voices united, a testament grew,
A proclamation of hope, a message to share,
In the temple's embrace, love was laid bare.

In Mary's arms, the Christ child lay,
A convergence of destinies, a dawning ray,
In Simeon's embrace, a blessing profound,
Anna's spirit rejoicing, love's presence found.

Meditation: Reflect on the profound impact of this moment within the temple—a convergence of faith, revelation, and destiny. Envision Simeon's and Anna's voices as they echo through the temple's sacred halls, proclaiming a message of hope, belief, and the fulfillment of God's promises.

GUIDED BY STARS – MATTHEW 2:1-12

Beneath the canvas of night's velvety cloak,
A star burst forth, its brilliance bespoke,
Magi from distant lands, their hearts stirred,
Following its light, a destiny's word.

From the East they came, a caravan's quest,
Guided by heavens, a purpose professed,
"Where is the newborn King?" they inquired,
Their question a spark, a prophecy inspired.

To Jerusalem's streets, their steps did lead,
Seeking a child, a Savior indeed,
Herod, troubled by news unknown,
Inquired of scribes, with a heart overthrown.

A prophecy revealed, Bethlehem's name,
A town of kings, where Messiah came,
To the city's outskirts, the Magi pressed,
Guided by the star, on their quest to invest.

In a humble abode, the starlight did gleam,
The Christ child's presence, a celestial dream,
They knelt in reverence, their gifts they bestowed,
Gold, frankincense, myrrh, love's offerings flowed.

In a dream, warned not to return by Herod's hand,
The Magi departed to their distant land,
A different route taken, their journey redirected,
Their hearts forever marked; a promise connected.

Meditation: Reflect on the significance of the Magi's journey—a pilgrimage guided by the stars, their steps orchestrated by the heavens themselves. Imagine their offerings, the reverence in their gestures, and the redirection of their faith. Contemplate the profound impact of their encounter with the Christ child—an encounter marked by destiny, faith, and the eternal promise that their journey unveils.

Refuge in the Shadows – *Matt. 2:13-18*

In the shadow of night, a dream took hold,
Joseph, a guardian, his heart unrolled,
"Arise," the angel's voice, a whisper's plea,
"Take the child and His mother, to Egypt flee."

A tyrant's fear, a threat to bear,
Herod's decree, a darkening air,
A massacre planned, innocent lives to take,
Innocence to be shattered, hearts to break.

Joseph obeyed, his heart's burden heavy,
In the quiet of night, he led his family,
To Egypt's safety, a refuge sought,
A journey of shadows, a danger fraught.

In a foreign land, amidst uncertainty,
Mary and Joseph held their child closely,
A family in exile, guided by grace,
Trusting in God's presence, seeking a safe place.

But in Bethlehem's streets, a tragedy grim,
A voice of mourning, a hope growing dim,
Rachel wept for her children, a cry to the skies,
A tale of loss and anguish, in Herod's guise.

Meditation: Contemplate the dichotomy of refuge and tragedy—Joseph's obedience leading his family to safety, while Bethlehem experiences heart-wrenching loss. Envision the shadows that envelop these events, a reminder of the complexities of life's tapestry, where moments of grace and suffering are interwoven.

Return from Exile – *Matt. 2:19-23/Luke 2:39*

In the quiet of night, a dream's gentle breeze,
An angel's whisper, carried on unseen seas,
"Arise," the voice urged, Joseph's heart stirred,
"Return to Israel, for danger's no longer heard."

From Egypt's refuge, a journey anew,
A path homeward, a sky's vibrant hue,
Mary and Joseph, with their child by their side,
Guided by dreams, in faith they'd confide.

But upon their return, a new threat did loom,
Archelaus reigned, Herod's heir in the room,
In dreams again warned, Joseph turned aside,
To Galilee's haven, a town to abide.

Nazareth, the destination, a humble retreat,
A haven of peace, a home so sweet,
In this simple abode, a promise held tight,
The Christ child's story, shining in the night.

Meditation: Think about the journey of return—a transition from exile to a new beginning. Picture the beauty of this transition, guided by dreams and angelic whispers. Reflect on the significance of Nazareth, where the Christ child's story continues to unfold, a story that shines brightly even in the quiet embrace of a humble home.

Growing in Grace – Luke 2:40-52

In Nazareth's embrace, a child did dwell,
Jesus, the Savior, in whom stories would swell,
Growing in wisdom, stature, and grace,
A divine journey, a destined embrace.

From infancy's innocence to childhood's bloom,
In Mary's care, love's gentle loom,
A boy of wonder, a heart pure and kind,
In carpenter's hands, a future aligned.

Year by year, a life unfolding bright,
In God's favor and human delight,
In the temple's halls, questions took flight,
A glimpse of purpose, a future's sight.

"Did you not know?" young Jesus asked,
A boy's inquiry, a truth unmasked,
In the father's house, a connection found,
A path of destiny, on holy ground.

In Nazareth's streets, His hands would learn,
Carpentry's art, love's fire to burn,
A life well lived, an example grand,
Guided by God's love, at Mary's hand.

Meditation: Contemplate the entirety of this journey—a life marked by growth, learning, and the intertwining of the human and divine. Imagine Jesus, a child who grows in wisdom and stature, guided by God's love, shaping a path that will ultimately fulfill a destiny of salvation and grace.

Wisdom's Temple – Luke 2:41-50

In Jerusalem's bustling streets, a feast aglow,
A yearly tradition, a pilgrimage's flow,
Mary, Joseph, and Jesus, a family in stride,
To the temple they journeyed, hearts open wide.

Days passed in celebration, in prayers' embrace,
The feast's splendor, the temple's grace,
But as the caravan turned to head home,
Jesus lingered behind, in the temple to roam.

Mary and Joseph, hearts heavy with care,
Returned to seek Him, a bond to repair,
Three days of searching, anxiety's hold,
Until in the temple's halls, His presence they'd behold.

"Son, why have you done this?" Mary cried,
In tender concern, love's worry belied,
"Did you not know?" Jesus replied, His gaze bright,
"I must be about my father's business, the truth's light."

In those sacred walls, wisdom unfurled,
In the temple's embrace, a destiny swirled,
A glimpse of purpose, a heart's devotion,
In Jesus' words, a divine notion.

Meditation: Think of the scene in the temple—the exchange between Mary, Joseph, and Jesus. Envision this moment as a revelation of wisdom, devotion, and divine purpose. Reflect on the powerful nature of human relationships and divine calling, a testament to the intricate tapestry of faith and destiny.

The Carpenter's Son – *Luke 2:51-52*

In Nazareth's embrace, a quiet abode,
Lived Jesus, in silence, the Promised One,
Years passed by, hidden from view,
In Mary's care, love's journey he'd pursue.

Obedience and honor, to parents he'd show,
In wisdom's shadow, humility would grow,
The carpenter's trade, his hands would mold,
As the mysteries of life and faith he'd unfold.

In favor with God and humanity's throng,
In Nazareth's streets, he'd belong,
A life well lived, a path set right,
In the Carpenter's hands, love's divine light.

Meditation: Picture the scene in Nazareth—the carpenter's son engaged in daily life, yet always guided by divine purpose. Envision a life shaped by wisdom, humility, and love—a life which embodies the Carpenter's hands shaping not only wood but also souls, illuminating the world with the brilliance of God's grace.

Chapter 2: The Voice of the Wilderness

Within the pages of the Gospels, a figure emerges whose life and message resonate across time and faiths—a harbinger of hope, a beacon of redemption, John the Baptist, a towering figure in the biblical narrative, stands as a symbol of profound transformation and the unyielding power of the redemptive aspects of God.

These poems, woven with reverence and contemplation, reflect upon various pivotal moments in the life of John the Baptist as recounted in the Gospels. With each stanza, each verse, they delve into the essence of her purpose—calling humanity to repentance, preparing hearts for the arrival of Christ, and embodying the struggle for righteousness in the face of power and adversity.

As we delve into these reflections, may we find ourselves drawn into the depths of redemption's call, resonating with John's message, and experiencing the transformation it brings. Just as he pointed the way to Christ, these poems guide us toward a greater understanding of the enduring relevance of his teachings, offering a timeless perspective on the redemptive journey that defines the greatest aspects of the human spirit.

An Outcrying Voice – Mark 1:1-4

In desert's expanse, where the wild winds roam,
A prophet emerges, his heart a holy home,
A voice crying out in the wilderness vast,
Announcing the One whose coming is cast.

Clothed in camel's hair, with leather-bound frame,
John takes his stand, his mission aflame,
He preaches of repentance, a baptism of grace,
Preparing hearts for the Savior's embrace.

His voice echoes loudly, a herald's refrain,
"Prepare the way, make straight the terrain,
The One who is mightier, whose presence draws near,
Will baptize with Spirit, casting out fear."

People flock to his side, their hearts open wide,
Confessing their sins, casting aside pride,
Into the Jordan's embrace, they step through the flow,
Washed in its waters, a new life they know.

A message resounding, in the wilderness clear,
John's proclamation reaches every ear,
A call to return, to be cleansed and renewed,
As God's kingdom approaches, hearts are subdued.

Meditation: Contemplate the themes of renewal, transformation, and preparation. Reflect on your own spiritual journey—how might the events described in the poem resonate with your desire for deeper connection and transformation?

Igniting the Soul – Mark 1:2-8

In wilderness vast, a voice does cry,
John, humble herald, his purpose held high,
A voice distinct, piercing the quiet air,
Calling hearts to heed, to prepare and declare.

A voice in the wilderness, a call to the soul,
Amidst barren landscapes, his message takes toll,
A message of readiness, hearts to be bared,
A path to be cleared, for the Divine to be shared.

Prepare the way, make the journey straight,
Within the soul's chambers, clear pathways await,
Removing obstacles, old patterns that bind,
Creating a space for the Sacred to find.

A baptism of repentance, a cleansing within,
The Jordan's embrace, where souls do begin,
Confessing transgressions, seeking to be free,
In the river's currents, grace's gentle decree.

But one mightier comes, beyond John's embrace,
A presence divine, filling every space,
Acknowledging humility, bowing with awe,
Recognizing the essence of a higher law.

Baptism of fire, Holy Spirit's embrace,
A refining force, igniting the grace,
Purifying the soul, transforming it whole,
Empowering the journey toward a celestial goal.

Water and Spirit, a dance of the two,
Symbolic immersion, a life to renew,
In John's proclamation, in the river's flow,
A narrative of transformation, a sacred echo.

Meditation: Think about the significance of fire as a symbol of both purification and inspiration. Reflect on how the themes of repentance, forgiveness, and encountering the Holy Spirit converge in this vivid imagery.

A Refining Fire – Matthew 3:11-12

In the wilderness's hush, John does proclaim,
Of One who follows, a mightier name,
He baptizes with water, a symbol of change,
But One comes with fire, a destiny rearranged.

John's hands may baptize with water's embrace,
But One arrives with fire's fervent grace,
A baptism of Spirit, a refining, divine,
Igniting souls' depths, where purpose aligns.

A winnowing fan in the hand of the Lord,
A separating force, truth to be restored,
Wheat from the chaff, the essence laid bare,
In fire's embrace, a cleansing to share.

The wheat, gathered to barn's safe embrace,
Nurtured and cherished, in love's endless grace,
Chaff to be burned, its purpose fulfilled,
In fire's purifying, its destiny instilled.

The winnowing fan's rhythm, the wind's whispered call,
A metaphor vivid, encompassing all,
The fire of truth, the Spirit's embrace,
A path of transformation, a soul's destined space.

Meditation: Contemplate how the imagery of fire is used here. It has dual aspects as both a purifying force and a separator, metaphorically representing the refining process that occurs within heart and soul.

The Prophet's Voice – *Matthew 14:4-12*

In a palace's shadow, a prophet does stand,
John the Baptist, a voice in the land,
A preacher of truth, fearless and bold,
A message of repentance, stories of old.

Herod's edicts transgressed, boundaries crossed,
For John spoke against, a truth unembossed,
He called for repentance, for hearts to be pure,
In a world marred by sin, a message to endure.

Herod's intrigue ensnared him, a dance of the court,
John's voice challenging, a royal rapport,
Yet Herod's regard held reverence, true,
In John's words, a prophet's truth drew.

A banquet, a daughter's dance, a promise unwise,
Herod's oath spoken, a plot's thin disguise,
Herodias's demand, a prophet's end sought,
John's life extinguished, truth's battle fought.

Beheaded in prison, a prophet's last breath,
A voice silenced by power, the cost of truth's death,
Yet John's legacy lingers, his message prevails,
In repentance's call, in salvation's trails.

Meditation: Reflect on the challenges faced by truth-bearers, the clash between power and righteousness, and the enduring impact of John's message of repentance.

Chapter 3: The Dawn of Transformation

In the heart of the Gospels lies a pivotal chapter, one that ushers in the beginning of Jesus Christ's transformative ministry. As we turn our gaze to this unfolding narrative, we are met with the emergence of Jesus as a powerful and compassionate figure, a teacher and healer whose actions and teachings would shape the course of human history.

In the poems that follow, we delve into the series of events that mark the commencement of Jesus' ministry. Each verse encapsulates a distinct moment, capturing the essence of the encounters, teachings, and miracles that heralded a new era of divine revelation. From the baptism in the Jordan River to the momentous conversations with Nicodemus, the narrative unfolds with vivid detail, inviting us to witness the profound significance of these early steps.

I have intended these poems to serve as both windows and mirrors, allowing us to peer into the past while reflecting on the enduring relevance of Jesus' ministry in our lives today. Through this exploration, we encounter themes of redemption, faith, healing, and the unbreakable bond between humanity and the divine. As Jesus steps forward to embrace his purpose, we witness the promise of salvation taking shape, the light of hope shining brightly in a world yearning for renewal.

Join us as we traverse these sacred themes, drawing wisdom and inspiration from the profound moments that set the stage for the transformative journey of Christ, the embodiment of love, grace, and the eternal promise of salvation.

The Lamb of God — John 1:29-34

Beside the Jordan's gentle flow,
A crowd did gather, hearts aglow,
John, the Baptist, his voice did proclaim,
"The Lamb of God!" he declared His name.

Behold the Messiah, the Chosen One,
Whose presence on Earth had just begun,
The sin-bearer, the Redeemer's grace,
In Jesus' arrival, a holy embrace.

"Before me He comes," John did say,
A greater than I, in a humble way,
A baptism of Spirit, a promise so grand,
In Jesus' presence, salvation's hand.

A dove from heaven, a Spirit's descent,
A sign divine, God's blessing sent,
Resting upon Him, the Chosen One,
Confirmation of purpose, God's own Son.

In John's voice resounds a witness clear,
"The Son of God!" for all to hear,
In humble obedience, he proclaimed the way,
The Lamb of God, the light of day.

Meditation: Contemplate John's role as a witness of Jesus' divinity. How do we do this in our daily lives? Think about the symbolism of the Lamb of God, and the significance of Jesus' baptism as a pivotal moment in His ministry.

Temptation and Triumph – *Matthew 4:1-11*

In the wilderness's quiet expanse,
Jesus walked, engaged in a sacred dance,
Forty days and nights, fasting alone,
A battle of wills, a trial of His own.

A tempter approached, his voice a lure,
"Command these stones," his intentions impure,
Yet Jesus stood firm, His purpose held tight,
"In God's Word alone, I find my delight."

To the pinnacle's height, the tempter led,
"Throw yourself down," his words widespread,
But Jesus resisted, His trust unswayed,
"In testing God's grace, I won't be waylaid."

Lastly, the world's kingdoms, their glory displayed,
"All shall be yours," the tempter conveyed,
But Jesus declared, "Worship God alone,"
In truth and devotion, His faith fully known.

With that, the tempter departed in haste,
Angels drew near, in the wilderness's space,
They ministered to Him, a triumphant scene,
In victory's embrace, God's purpose was gleaned.

Meditation: Reflect on Jesus' unwavering commitment to God's will, His triumph over temptation, and the significance of relying on Scripture as a source of strength and guidance.

Invitation and Revelation – *John 1:35-51*

Beside the Jordan's flowing stream,
Two disciples followed, a sacred dream,
John the Baptist pointed, "Behold the Lamb,"
Jesus walked by, the great "I AM."

"Rabbi," they called, their hearts alight,
"Where do you dwell?" inquired the night,
"Come and see," His response so clear,
An invitation to draw near.

Nathanael came, skepticism in his voice,
"Can anything good come?" he questioned, a choice,
But Jesus knew him, beyond the eyes' gaze,
A fig tree encounter, faith ablaze.

Amazed, Nathanael professed in haste,
"You are the Son of God!" he embraced,
Jesus promised greater things yet to see,
Heaven's realm opened, divine mystery.

A wedding in Cana, a lack of wine,
Mary's concern, a plan divine,
Water to wine, a miracle's birth,
Faith's foundation, a life's new worth.

To Nicodemus, in shadows of night,
Jesus spoke of rebirth, of spiritual light,
Born of water and spirit, anew to begin,
The kingdom's entry, a truth within.

To the Samaritan woman, by Jacob's well,
Jesus offered living water to quell,
A conversation deep, her heart transformed,
Messiah revealed, her life reformed.

From afar, a royal official did plead,
His son near death, his desperation's need,
"Go, your son lives," Jesus declared,
A miracle's touch, a father's prayers shared.

Two days later, his son's health restored,
Faith's journey complete, God's grace poured,
In each encounter, lives transformed anew,
Jesus revealed, God's love in view.

Meditation: This poem highlights the themes of human faith, revelation, and the life-changing nature of encountering the Son of God. Reflect upon the power of Jesus' invitation to "come and see," His ability to see beyond the surface and know our hearts, and the transformative impact of encountering Him.

The Miracle of Transformation — *John 2:1-11*

In Cana's town, where joy filled the night,
A wedding was held 'neath lantern light.
Mary leaned close, her voice hushed and shy—
"They've run out of wine," was her quiet cry.

Jesus and disciples, in attendance there,
A mother's request, a moment to share,
"Fill the jars with water," He said,
Obedience followed, a miracle ahead.

Water to wine, a transformation grand,
Quality surpassed, the best at hand,
A symbol of grace, abundance untold,
Jesus' power displayed, a story to be told.

Meditation: Think on the themes of transformation, abundance, and the divine power of Jesus as He turns water into wine. Consider the significance of this miracle in revealing Jesus' identity and the symbolism of water turning into wine as representation of grace and abundance.

THE CLEANSING OF THE TEMPLE – *JOHN 2:12-22*

Jerusalem's temple, a place of devotion,
A gathering of souls, a sacred emotion,
Passover observed, a significant time,
Jesus arrived, with purpose sublime.

Merchants and moneychangers, a bustling trade,
In the temple's courtyard, their wares displayed,
Jesus observed, a righteous dismay,
A moment to cleanse, a point to convey.

Cords fashioned into a whip, a righteous zeal,
Tables overturned, a message to reveal,
"Stop making my Father's house a den of trade,"
Jesus declared, a truth to cascade.

Meditation: This poem emphasizes Jesus' righteous anger and his determination to restore the sanctity of the temple. Reflect on the significance of Jesus' actions in confronting the misuse of a sacred space and asserting the importance of true worship.

The Knowing Hearts – *John 2:23-25*

In Jerusalem's midst, a Passover's glow,

Crowds gathered, devotion in hearts' flow,

Signs and wonders, Jesus did display,

Yet belief's depth, He perceived his own way.

Many believed, drawn by miracles grand,

In Jesus' name, they'd come to stand,

Yet He perceived the hearts' secret truth,

Their faith's foundation, their belief's root.

Human hearts, their motives He knew,

The depth of conviction, to Him not askew,

In the midst of acclaim, he'd withhold,

For in true faith's fire, he'd unfold.

Meditation: Think about the importance of genuine faith and the fact that Jesus can see beyond outward appearances to the true state of the heart.

Born Anew – *John 3:1-21*

In shadows' embrace, a seeker did tread,
Nicodemus by name, a questioning spread,
Under cover of night, his inquiry keen,
To Jesus he came, a truth to glean.

"Born anew," Jesus proclaimed with grace,
A rebirth of spirit, a divine embrace,
Water and Spirit, He made known,
A transformation deep, a truth shown.

Marvel not at these words, Jesus did say,
For salvation's essence, I'll now convey,
A Son sent with love, the world to save,
Believe in his name, eternal life pave.

Darkness exposed by the light's pure glow,
Truth's unveiled, and hearts will know,
In the light's presence, deeds shall stand,
Or hide in darkness, from truth's demand.

Meditation: Contemplate this well-known story but with a fresh perspective. Can you see through Nicodemus' eyes? Think about the themes of rebirth, salvation, and the contrast between light and darkness in the spiritual journey.

Rivers of Faith – *John 3:22-36*

Beside the Jordan's flow, a scene did unfold,
Disciples of John, and Jesus, stories retold,
Baptisms anew, a sacred rite,
In waters' embrace, hearts took flight.

A question arose, disciples' concern,
"Rabbi, the man you've taught, we discern,
He too baptizes, and followers gather near,
Is this a cause for worry, a cause for fear?"

John's response humble, his purpose clear,
"I rejoice in his rise, no threat do I hear,
A voice for the groom, the bridegroom's delight,
Decreasing am I, to his greater light."

From heaven above, the Son of God came,
To share God's message, salvation's aim,
Believe in Him, eternal life obtain,
Rejecting his light, darkness remains.

Meditation: With this poem we delve into John's humility. Think about his recognition of Jesus' divine role and the call to believe in the Son of God for eternal life.

Samaritan Encounter – *John 4:1-4*

In Samaria's land, a journey begun,
Jesus departed, a task to be done,
Leaving Judea's roads, for Galilee's reach,
A journey through Samaria, a lesson to teach.

Baptizing not Jesus, but his disciples did,
In waters' embrace, a purpose well hid,
A rising not from Jesus, but from God above,
A ministry unfolding, a message of love.

Meditation: Contemplate Jesus' unconventional route and the subtle purpose behind the journey, hinting at the unfolding ministry and message of divine love.

Thirst Quenched – *John 4:5-42*

By Jacob's well, in the noonday heat,
A Samaritan woman, a heart to meet,
Drawn to water's source, her jar to fill,
Unaware of the purpose, of a thirst to still.

Jesus sat weary, disciples away,
He asked for a drink, a conversation's sway,
A conversation taboo, a cultural line,
Yet Jesus crossed boundaries, a love divine.

He offered living water, a metaphor deep,
A spiritual truth, secrets to reap,
The woman puzzled, her heart's yearning stirred,
A thirst for more than earthly water incurred.

Revealing her life's story, her choices laid bare,
Jesus saw her soul, her burdens to share,
A revelation dawned, her heart did sing,
Could He be the Messiah, the long-awaited King?

Returning to town, her testimony spilled,
Come meet a man, her heart's desire fulfilled,
Could He be the Christ, the Savior true?
A message of hope, a promise to pursue.

The townsmen came, their curiosity piqued,
They met Jesus, and the truth they'd seek,
A Savior among them, their hearts to embrace,
Belief ignited, redemption's grace.

Meditation: Reflect upon the transformative effect of encountering the Messiah. Think upon the themes of how we, as believers, should cross social boundaries and pursue inner transformation through the word of God.

Returning Faith – John 4:43-45

From Sychar to Galilee, Jesus embarked,
A journey through time, faith's spark,
Back to Cana, where water to wine He turned,
A town that once witnessed miracles earned.

Greeted by welcome, a memory revived,
For in Cana's soil, belief had thrived,
A nobleman sought, his son at the brink,
Desperate for healing, for life's link.

He heard of Jesus, of signs performed,
Of miracles heralded, of truth affirmed,
To Cana he journeyed, his heart's plea sincere,
With faith as his guide, his hope clear.

"Come quickly," he urged, his son's fate severe,
For life hung in balance, death drawing near,
But Jesus's words reassured his quest,
"Go, your son lives," a promise blessed.

Returning home, his servants met,
News of his son's recovery, a truth set,
At the very hour Jesus declared,
His faith confirmed, his heart repaired

Meditation: Think upon the themes contained within this story: the essence of faith and its affirmation, as the nobleman's belief transforms into a reality. The theme of healing and the connection between faith and miracles are central to this reflection.

Chapter 4: Radiant Lights in the North

The collection of poems in this chapter presents a vivid and insightful depiction of Jesus' Northern Ministry period, a critical phase in the earthly journey. This marked a shift in His ministry as He ventured beyond familiar regions and embarked on a journey of spreading His teachings, healing, and performing miracles. These poems capture various episodes from this period, shedding light on both the profound teachings and the powerful deeds that unfolded during this time.

This chapter emphasizes Jesus' connection with the natural world and his ability to find spiritual lessons in everyday experiences. The imagery of fishing, harvesting, and sowing seeds in the poems draw parallels between physical processes and spiritual truths. This approach not only resonated with his audience's everyday lives but also reinforced the idea that God's kingdom is present in the ordinary as well as the extraordinary.

This period was marked by diverse encounters, miracles, and parables which continue to inspire and guide individuals on their own spiritual journeys. Through these poems, I invite you to connect with the essence of Jesus' ministry, reflect on its enduring relevance, and find inspiration in His teachings and actions.

FAITH'S HEALING TOUCH – *JOHN 4:46-54*

In Capernaum's streets, a nobleman's plea,
An official's heart weighed by his son's misery,
"Come heal," he entreated, faith's cry to impart,
To Jesus, the healer, a father's longing heart.

"Unless you see signs, you won't believe," he heard,
Jesus' words echoed, a truth's whispered word,
The father's resolve unwavering, faith's choice,
"Come before my child's death, restore his voice."

"Go, your son lives," Jesus replied,
In those words, a promise, a father's guide,
The official's faith deepened, his steps affirmed,
Homeward he journeyed, where healing was confirmed.

On the journey's path, his servants met,
"Your son lives!" they exclaimed, no more to fret,
The fever subsided, the healing begun,
In a father's faith, redemption's story won.

Meditation: This poem takes us on a journey of faith, from the pleas for healing to the ultimate redemption brought about by Jesus' words. Reflect on the power of unwavering faith and the transformative touch of Jesus' healing grace.

Proclamation and Rejection – *Luke 4:16-30*

In Nazareth's synagogue, a hometown's pride,
Jesus stood tall, the scroll unrolled wide,
Isaiah's words chosen, a prophecy declared,
"The Spirit anointed me," a truth He shared.

Eyes fixed on Him, anticipation's hum,
In his voice, the words of the prophet's sum,
"The captive's release, the blind made to see,
Good news proclaimed, for the oppressed and free."

Amazement followed, whispers filled the air,
"Isn't this Joseph's son?" a question laid bare,
Yet Jesus perceived their thoughts, their doubts unveiled,
A prophet's wisdom, a Savior's truth exhaled.

He spoke of Elijah and the widow's embrace,
A Gentile's grace received in God's sacred space,
The people's hearts stirred, a rising tide,
But in their midst, skepticism would collide.

A prophet's honor withheld, rejection's sting,
From admiration to anger, truths unwring,
"To other towns," Jesus spoke, destiny's thread,
Yet on the precipice, they sought his life's shred.

They led Him to a cliff, a precipice's brink,
But Jesus passed through, a life left to think,
In rejection's shadow, his mission unfurled,
A Savior's calling, redemption's world.

Meditation: These verses explore the tension between admiration and rejection, to showcase Jesus' role as prophet and savior. Reflect upon the complexities of acceptance and rejection in the face of truth and transformation.

The Seeds of Truth – *Mark 4:13-20*

Beside the sea's shore, a crowd did gather,
Jesus spoke in parables, truth he'd tether,
"The Sower sows," his tale did begin,
A story of seeds, a truth within.

The seed on the path, devoured, snatched away,
By doubt and disbelief, led astray,
The rocky ground, a shoot springs fast,
But withers in trials, faith doesn't last.

Among thorns, the seed struggles to rise,
Choked by worries, by worldly ties,
Yet the seed on good soil, deep roots it finds,
Fruitful and flourishing, truth in its binds.

The crowd listened, pondered, hearts in quest,
Yet the disciples, seeking to be blessed,
Sought deeper meanings, a secret untold,
Jesus explained, truth to unfold.

The seeds are the Word, the message divine,
The hearts are the soil, where truth does shine,
Doubt, distractions, life's trials arise,
But in receptive hearts, truth never dies.

Meditation: Reflect on the different types of soil that represent the receptivity of human hearts to the message of the truth. This parable invites us to reflect on the condition of our hearts and our responsiveness to the seeds of divine wisdom.

CASTING NETS OF FAITH – *MATTHEW 4:18-22*

Beside Galilee's shore, a scene did unfold,
Jesus walking, disciples bold,
Two brothers, Simon and Andrew by name,
Fishing the waters, their trade's ancient claim.

"Follow me," Jesus called, his voice clear,
"Become fishers of men, have no fear,"
They left their nets, a journey anew,
A purpose ignited, a truth to pursue.

Further down the shore, James and John,
Mending their nets, as day's light shone,
"Come," Jesus beckoned, a summons divine,
Leaving their father, their purpose did align.

With hearts set afire, they followed his lead,
Leaving behind all, the nets and the creed,
To be fishers of men, to spread truth's embrace,
In discipleship's journey, they found their place.

Meditation: These verses capture the pivotal moment when Simon, Andrew, James and John leave their livelihoods to follow Jesus to become fishers of men. This story should prompt us to reflect on the courage and trust required to answer a divine call and embark on a transformative journey of faith.

Authority Unveiled – *Luke 4:31-37*

In Capernaum's synagogue, a crowd did gather,
Jesus taught with authority, his voice a lather,
Amazement filled hearts, his words so profound,
Demons trembled, truth's power unbound.

A man possessed, a demon's grip tight,
Cried out in fear, in the holy light,
"Be silent!" Jesus commanded, his voice stern,
The demon obeyed, a lesson to learn.

Witnesses marveled, a teaching anew,
Words with authority, demons they slew,
Rumors spread fast, his fame taking flight,
Authority unveiled, a beacon of light.

In the synagogue's walls, a scene did unfold,
The power of Jesus, a story retold,
In his teaching, in his presence, a truth resounded,
Authority and grace, his message astounded.

Meditation: This story delves into the awe-inspiring impact of Jesus' teaching and the revelation of divine authority. It invites us to consider the transformative power of truth and the recognition of Jesus as the source of ultimate authority.

Healing Touch – *Mark 1:29-34*

In Simon's home, a fever burned bright,
Simon's mother-in-law lay, gripped by its might,
Word spread fast, the news did unfold,
Jesus approached; a healer untold.

With compassion's touch, He reached her side,
The fever left, her health was allied,
She rose from her bed, a miracle's trace,
Grateful, she served, her heart full of grace.

As evening descended, a crowd did throng,
The sick and possessed, their need so strong,
Jesus healed many, their ailments He knew,
Demons silenced, his power they drew.

But silence He commanded, a secret to keep,
For the time had not come, his mission so deep,
The healer's touch, a glimpse of his reign,
Compassion and power, a world to reclaim.

Meditation: This poem reflects on the transformative power of Jesus' healing touch and the balance between his compassion and the necessity of keeping his identity as Messiah a secret for a time. It invites us to consider the dual nature of Jesus as both a healer and a bearer of a greater mission.

A Healing Light – *Matthew 4:23-25*

Beside Galilee's shores, a scene aglow,
Jesus moved among them, a healing flow,
Proclaiming the Gospel, a message of grace,
The sick and afflicted sought his embrace.

Healing every disease, restoring the whole,
A healing light, a compassion-filled soul,
From villages and towns, a multitude came,
Drawn by his touch, their lives never the same.

Paralytics walked, the blind regained sight,
Deaf ears opened wide, darkness turned to light,
Afflictions released, the demon-possessed free,
A foretaste of Kingdom, a glimpse of what will be.

News spread like wildfire, across the land,
People from afar, their hopes in his hand,
Syria, Decapolis, a multitude swarmed,
Seeking the healer, their lives transformed.

Meditation: A common theme in the ministry of Jesus is the emphasis of His healing touch and the widespread recognition of his miraculous powers. Contemplate how these actions also symbolize the spiritual healing and restoration Jesus offers to all who seek Him.

An Unclean Cry – Mark 1:40-45

A leper's plea, a cry of despair,
Seeking release from affliction's snare,
"Lord, if you will," the leper implored,
His hope anchored in Jesus, his heart restored.

Moved by compassion, Jesus reached out,
His touch breaking barriers, dispelling doubt,
"I will," He declared, a promise fulfilled,
The leper's skin cleared, his heart stilled.

"Be cleansed," the command, a word of might,
Instantly the leprosy vanished from sight,
A transformation profound, a healing embrace,
In that sacred moment, love's healing grace.

But Jesus' stern words echoed, a command to keep,
Silent witness, secrets deep,
The leper disobeyed, sharing his cure,
A proclamation that would allure.

The news spread wide, the crowds flocked near,
A healer like none, compassion clear,
Yet Jesus withdrew, to deserted places he'd roam,
A mission unfolding, a purpose to enthrone.

Meditation: There is a significance to the leper's proclamation and once again we see the tension highlighted between Jesus' desire for privacy and his growing fame. Contemplate how in this instance, Jesus' healing serves as a symbol of the transformative power of Christ's love and mercy, and how, with Him by your side, you can never be 'unclean.'

FAITH'S UNVEILING – *LUKE 5:17-26*

In a house teeming with expectant eyes,
A paralytic lay, his spirit's cries,
Crowded room, roof's disruption, a daring feat,
A spectacle before Jesus' seat.

Faith's conviction displayed, friends took hold,
Lowering the man, a story to be told,
Jesus saw their faith, a heart's plea,
Forgiveness granted; spirit set free.

Religious leaders questioned, hearts stirred,
Blasphemy they heard, their thoughts incurred,
But Jesus, perceiving their doubt-filled mind,
A challenge posed, truth to find.

"Which is easier, to forgive or heal?"
A probing question, a truth to reveal,
Both acts divine, grace unmeasured,
To doubt the power, faith's treasure.

A command issued, "Rise, take your bed,"
Instantly the paralytic's limbs he'd spread,
Walking forth, spirit renewed,
A miracle witnessed; faith pursued.

Astounded crowds, glorifying God's name,
Witnessing a miracle's flame,
In that house, faith's unveiling displayed,
A paralytic's life forever remade.

Meditation: This story highlights the faith of the friends who brought the paralytic to Jesus and the depth of their belief which led them to disrupt the roof. Think about the other emphasis in this story—Jesus' power to forgive as well as heal and the challenge He posed to the religious leaders' understanding. This story of healing further serves as a testament to the transformative power of faith and Christ's authority.

The Call of Transformation – *Matthew 9:9-13*

At a tax collector's booth, a scene set,
A man named Matthew, a life in debt,
A call resounding, "Follow me," Christ's voice,
An invitation to change, a destiny's choice.

Leaving his post, Matthew obeyed,
A table left behind, debts unpaid,
A feast he hosted, a gathering grand,
Sinners and outcasts, a diverse band.

Pharisees questioned, criticism thrown,
"Why eat with sinners?" their disdain shown,
Jesus' response, a message profound,
"I desire mercy, not sacrifice," he'd expound.

The sick need healing, the lost a guide,
Compassion's call, a heart opens wide,
A call of transformation, a life anew,
Matthew's story, a testament true.

Meditation: This is the pivotal moment where Jesus calls Matthew, a tax collector, to follow Him. Think about how the nature of this story explores the transformative power of Christ's call, as Matthew leaves his old life behind and becomes a disciple. Contemplate the significance of Jesus' association with sinners and outcasts, emphasizing his message of mercy and compassion.

NEW WINE, NEW WINESKINS – MARK 2:18-22

Amidst fasting and prayers, a question posed,
"Why don't your disciples fast?" they supposed,
Jesus' response, a parable's art,
New wine in new wineskins, a message to impart.

Wedding feasts and celebrations anew,
A joyous occasion, love's union in view,
The old and the new, a balance to find,
A shift in perspective, a truth intertwined.

As garments and wineskins, worn and old,
Cannot contain new, stories unfold,
A call to embrace change, a faith to renew,
In Christ's teaching, a lesson so true.

Mediation: This story delves into the exchange between Jesus and the Pharisees regarding fasting, weaving in the parable of new wine and old wineskins. Reflect on the need for open hearts and minds to embrace the transformative teachings of Christ, shedding the old to make room for the new.

THE LORD OF THE SABBATH – *Matthew 12:1-8*

In grain-filled fields, a scene unfolds,
Disciples plucking grain, as their journey holds,
Pharisees object, rules they uphold,
But Jesus' response, a truth untold.

Recalling David's need, a precedent set,
The sacred bread consumed, in hunger's debt,
The temple's priests, on the Sabbath, they serve,
A greater purpose, a truth to preserve.

"The Son of Man is Lord of the Sabbath," He claims,
A declaration resounds, in truth's flames,
A reminder of mercy over ritual's reign,
A lesson in grace, amid legalistic chain.

Meditation: Here we see another encounter between Christ and the Pharisees, this time in a grain field on the Sabbath. Think upon Jesus' exchange as He emphasizes the higher principles of mercy and compassion over rigid adherence to religious rules. Contemplate the balance between spiritual principles and legalistic practices.

The Withered is Restored – *Luke 6:6-11*

In a synagogue's hall, a man with a withered hand,
A test of compassion, as rules demand,
Pharisees watched, judgment in their eyes,
Would Jesus heal on the Sabbath, a question of ties?

Jesus, aware of their thoughts and intent,
A challenge He posed, a truth to present,
"Is it lawful to do good on the Sabbath?" He inquired,
A lesson in love, a perspective rewired.

With the man before them, Jesus stood,
Healing hand outstretched, misunderstood,
The man's hand restored, his heart filled with grace,
Yet Pharisees' anger painted their face.

A question He asked, a logic profound,
"Is it lawful to save life or let it be bound?"
No answer they gave, no truth they could find,
Their hearts closed to love, to a mercy aligned.

Meditation: This story encourages reflection on the balance between religious traditions and acts of love. Reflect upon the principle of doing good and showing mercy, even on a holy day.

Hope for the Broken – *Matthew 12:15-21*

Amidst the crowds that followed Him,
A healer's touch, a light not dim,
Jesus withdrew, his mercy clear,
Healing the sick, calming fear.

A prophecy fulfilled, Isaiah's word,
A servant's mission, compassion stirred,
A bruised reed He wouldn't break,
A smoldering wick, he'd ignite, awake.

Gentle yet powerful, hope he'd impart,
A Savior's touch, a wounded heart,
Nations would hope, in his name find,
The promise of redemption, love intertwined.

A message of justice, a truth to proclaim,
The gospel's song, a world to reclaim,
In his name, the Gentiles trust,
A Savior's love, forever robust.

Meditation: This story captures the essence of Jesus' compassionate healing and the fulfillment of the prophecy from Isaiah. Reflect on Jesus as a source of hope and restoration for the broken and marginalized. There is significance here in the mission to bring healing and hope to a hurting world.

Chosen Disciples – *Luke 6:12-16*

Beneath the expanse of a starlit night,
In solitude's embrace, out of sight,
Jesus sought the Father's face,
In prayerful communion, seeking grace.

Twelve were chosen, a circle small,
Disciples destined to heed his call,
Simon named Peter, a rock to be,
Andrew his brother, followers free.

James and John, sons of thunder's might,
Their fishing nets left, hearts set alight,
Philip and Bartholomew, faithful pair,
Thomas and Matthew, a diverse share.

James, son of Alphaeus, quiet and true,
Simon, the Zealot, in purpose grew,
Judas, the son of James, a steadfast heart,
And Judas Iscariot, whose betrayal would depart.

Chosen from many, destined to share,
In Christ's ministry, a burden to bear,
The twelve apostles, diverse and dear,
Their mission proclaimed, the Good News to steer.

Meditation: This is one of the most significant moments in the Gospels when Jesus selects the twelve apostles to be his chosen companions in his ministry. Reflect upon the diversity among the disciples and their common, shared mission to spread the Good News. Think upon the calling of the disciples and the roles they would play in furthering Jesus' message of love and salvation.

Sermon on the Mount – *Matt. 5:1-Matt.7:29*

Upon a mount, in nature's embrace,
A crowd gathered, a diverse grace,
Jesus, the Teacher, his voice did soar,
A sermon of truths, wisdom to explore.

"Blessed are the poor in spirit," He began,
A message of hope, a divine plan,
Meekness, mercy, hunger for right,
Words of comfort, in hearts took flight.

"You are the salt, the light of the earth,"
A call to shine, to show your worth,
Laws transformed, in love's true command,
A heart's intent, a divine stand.

"Love your enemies," a challenge profound,
Forgiveness's call, a grace unbound,
Prayer and fasting, in secret's repose,
A heart's devotion, God only knows.

"Ask, seek, knock," He encouraged them,
A promise of answers, when faith's a gem,
The golden rule, love others as self,
A wisdom's wealth, a spiritual health.

A house on rock, firm and secure,
Faith's foundation, steadfast and pure,
The crowd amazed, his teachings divine,
Authority's power, in every line.

Meditation: These verses focus on the essence of the sermon on the mount and on key lessons such as the Beatitudes, the call to be salt and light, love for enemies, prayer, and the golden rule. Contemplate these teachings and their timeless relevance in guiding believers to live out their faith with compassion, love, and steadfastness.

Faith That Moves Mountains – Luke 7:1-10

In Capernaum's midst, a centurion stood,
A man of influence, faith understood,
A servant beloved, sick and frail,
In Jesus' power, his hope set sail.

Word of the Teacher's might reached his ear,
A plea arose, dispelling all fear,
Though unworthy he felt, the centurion knew,
A word from Christ, healing anew.

"Lord, don't trouble yourself," he conveyed,
A heart of humility, in faith arrayed,
"Just say the word, my servant will live,
For I am under authority, I believe."

Amazed, Jesus turned to the crowd,
A marvel He found in faith's shroud,
"Not in Israel have I found such trust,"
He praised the centurion, faith robust.

His servant was healed in that very hour,
The centurion's faith, a radiant flower,
In this tale of trust, an example's set,
A faith that moves mountains, a heart's strong bet.

Meditation: These verses focus on the centurion's humble request and unwavering belief in Jesus' authority, which leads to the healing of his servant. Reflect on the power of faith and the profound impact it can have in our lives when we follow the example of the centurion.

Restoration Beyond Tears – *Luke 7:11-17*

In Nain's sorrowful streets, a funeral procession's flow,
A widow's heartache, a mother's woe,
Her only son, lifeless and still,
In death's embrace, a void to fill.

Jesus, the compassionate, drew near,
His heart stirred by grief's atmosphere,
He touched the bier, a gesture of grace,
"Arise," He spoke, life's chains to erase.

The young man arose, a miracle profound,
In Nain's midst, hope's sweet sound,
A widow's tears transformed to joy,
In Jesus' presence, grief's alloy.

The crowd was seized with awe's embrace,
Witnessing resurrection's grace,
"God has visited us," they proclaimed,
A Savior's touch, a life reclaimed.

Meditation: This story underscores the message that with Jesus, even in our most challenging situations, there is the possibility of restoration and joy beyond our expectations. Reflect upon the transformative nature of Christ's presence and the hope He brings to moments of sorrow and loss.

CONFIRMING HOPE – MATTHEW 11:2-9

In prison's shadow, doubts did creep,
John the Baptist, faith's doubts to sweep,
He sent his disciples, a message to bear,
"Are you the One?" in earnest prayer.

To Jesus they came, with John's query in hand,
"Are you the Expected?" they sought to understand,
Jesus' response was a testament clear,
"Go and report what you see and hear."

The blind receive sight, the lame walk with grace,
Lepers are cleansed, hope's smile on their face,
The deaf hear, the dead rise, and the poor are blessed,
In Jesus' ministry, God's love expressed.

Jesus turned to the crowd with words of acclaim,
Describing John's role in God's divine aim,
A prophet and more, a messenger true,
Preparing the way, a purpose in view.

Meditation: This story invites contemplation on the journey of faith and doubt that we all experience, and the ways which Jesus' response confirms hope and faith. It underscores the transformative power of witnessing the works of Jesus and the unique role John played in preparing the world for the Messiah's return.

Invitation to Rest – *Matthew 11:20-30*

In towns of Galilee, where Jesus trod,
His miracles proclaimed, the hand of God,
Yet cities remained unyielding, hearts stone,
Their stubbornness revealed, their fate known.

"Woe to you," Jesus spoke, a lament profound,
For Chorazin, Bethsaida, a destiny unbound,
Tyre and Sidon, repentance was due,
Sodom's fate gentler, in comparison's view.

To Capernaum, a plea directed,
The weight of privilege, the truth reflected,
Miracles witnessed, hearts unimpressed,
An invitation unheeded, a call suppressed.

Yet in this moment of sorrow, a promise shines,
A divine invitation, love's embrace entwines,
"Come to me, weary ones," Jesus implores,
A burden exchange, a rest that restores.

Learn from the gentle, the lowly in heart,
A yoke of love, grace's counterpart,
An invitation to find rest in His care,
A promise of solace, a refuge rare.

Meditation: Here Jesus laments the lack of response from various cities and extends an invitation to all who are weary and burdened. This poem invites reflection on the themes of repentance, privilege and finding rest in Christ amidst life's challenges.

A Sinner's Redemption – Luke 7:36-50

In a Pharisee's house, a table prepared,
A feast of stature, an event ensnared,
A sinful woman enters, her presence known,
Her actions a story, a heart's journey shown.

With an alabaster jar, tears freely flow,
Her tears bathe His feet, love's overflow,
With her hair, she dries, humility expressed,
An act of worship, a heart's request.

The Pharisee judges, his thoughts unvoiced,
But Jesus perceives, His love rejoiced,
A parable spoken, two debtors portrayed,
A lesson of gratitude, a lesson displayed.

Forgiveness abundant, the woman receives,
Her sins pardoned, her heart believes,
"Your faith has saved you," Jesus declared,
A sinner redeemed; a soul repaired.

Meditation: Reflect upon the themes of forgiveness, humility, and the transformative power of faith in Christ. Contemplate the contrast between the Pharisees' judgement and Christ's compassion, highlighting the woman's redemption through her sincere act of love and faith.

Divided Hearts – *Mark 3:20-30*

In a house crowded, a multitude near,
Family concerns, on Jesus, they peer,
"He is out of His mind," they whispered, concerned,
A public figure, His reputation discerned.

The scribes from Jerusalem, doubts they sowed,
"By Beelzebul's power," they boldly showed,
Accusing Jesus, His miracles claimed false,
A plot devised; an intention adverse.

Jesus, aware, their thoughts He perceived,
A kingdom divided, a message believed,
"How can Satan cast out Satan?" He said,
A kingdom imploded; a kingdom misled.

A stern warning given, a sin to blaspheme,
The Spirit's work mocked, a dangerous scheme,
A sin of eternal consequence revealed,
A heart divided; its fate now sealed

Meditation: This story prompts reflection on the gravity of blaspheming the Holy Spirit and the danger of a divided heart. It contrasts Jesus' defense of His actions with the scribes attempts to discredit Him, highlighting the ultimate importance of recognizing the spirit's work and maintaining a heart united in faith.

Seeking Signs – Matthew 12:38-45

Amid the crowd's clamor, voices entwined,
Pharisees approached, skeptics in kind,
"Teacher, show us a sign," they demanded with doubt,
Seeking a proof, their intentions devout.

Jesus rebuked their quest for a sign,
A wicked generation's heart in decline,
Like Jonah's tale, three days in the whale,
So would the Son of Man's story prevail.

The Queen of the South, her wisdom displayed,
She came to Solomon, a journey she made,
Yet here stood Wisdom, greater than a king,
Yet they refused belief, a truth puzzling.

An unclean spirit expelled, a man freed,
But the void within remained to impede,
Returning with friends, an even worse fate,
A house swept clean, a dismal state.

Meditation: This poem prompts contemplation on the nature of faith and skepticism, contrasting the Pharisees' quest for signs with Jesus' teachings about the state of the heart. The imagery of Jonah and the Queen of the South serves to illustrate this call for belief without the need for constant proof.

Family in Faith – Mark 3:31-35

Amidst the crowd's fervor, a message conveyed,
Word reached Jesus that family had stayed,
"Your mother and brothers," they spoke with care,
Seeking your presence, an embrace to share.

But Jesus expanded the circle of kin,
A lesson profound, a truth from within,
"Whoever does God's will," He proclaimed with grace,
Is family to me, a sacred embrace.

A bond forged not just by blood's decree,
But by faith's union, a love flowing free,
In the realm of God's purpose, a family is made,
By hearts bound in faith, love's serenade.

Meditation: Here Jesus expands his concept of family to include those who do God's will. This underscores the idea that faith is a powerful force that can connect individuals in a deeper and more profound way than mere lineage. Contemplate the spiritual bonds that unite believers as a family, transcending biological relationships.

Master of the Storm – Mark 4:35-41

On a boat, disciples embarked with trust,
A sea voyage begun, sails unfurled in gust,
But a tempest arose, waves fierce and wild,
Fear gripped their hearts, like an eerie child.

As water surged and winds did roar,
Jesus slept, undisturbed at the core,
"Master, do you not care?" they cried in despair,
The tempest's fury, more than they could bear.

With a rebuke, Jesus calmed the sea's rage,
His words held power, storms to assuage,
"Peace, be still!" He commanded, a voice so clear,
The tempest obeyed; the disciples drew near.

"Why are you afraid?" Jesus questioned their doubt,
"Where is your faith?" He inquired about,
Amidst the storm's fury, a lesson they learned,
That the Master of the storm, their trust had earned.

Meditation: This story speaks to the importance of trusting in the 'master of the storm' who has the power to bring peace amidst life's tumultuous challenges. Contemplate the power of faith during adversity, highlighting the disciples' fear and Jesus' authority over nature's forces.

LIBERATION OF THE TORMENTED – *LUKE 8:26-39*

In Gadarenes' land, a demon-possessed soul,
Haunted by torment, beyond control,
Chains couldn't bind him, his mind in despair,
In tombs he dwelled, a captive in layers.

Approaching the shore, Jesus stepped on land,
The tormented man met Him, with chains in hand,
"What have you to do with me, Son of God?" he cried,
The demons within him, their torment denied.

"Legion," they answered, their voices a choir,
Begging not to be sent to abyss's dire,
A herd of swine nearby, they beseeched to go,
Into them they entered, their fate to bestow.

The swine rushed into the sea, a watery grave,
The town's people witnessed, in awe and shockwave,
But the man, now free, sat at Jesus' feet,
Clothed and in sanity, his torment complete.

"Return home," Jesus bid him, his life restored,
To tell of God's mercy, his heart's praise poured,
The man became a witness, a testimony grand,
Of Jesus' liberation, in Gadarenes' land.

Meditation: This story highlights the restoration of a tormented soul and the subsequent role of that soul in sharing God's mercy and redemption. Reflect on Jesus' healing and deliverance, as well as the transformative impact of encountering the savior.

The Resurrected Life — Mark 5:21-43

In Capernaum's crowd, a ruler did plea,
Jairus by name, his daughter's life at sea,
Falling at Jesus' feet, his voice rang clear,
"Begone, ailment's shadow, let my daughter draw near."

Jesus, with compassion, agreed to the plea,
A throng followed them, curiosity's decree,
In the midst of the journey, a woman pressed near,
Twelve years in affliction, her heart filled with fear.

She reached for Jesus' cloak, a touch so slight,
Power surged from Him, her ailment took flight,
"Daughter, your faith healed you," Jesus declared,
In her touch, healing's secret lay bared.

Yet while the encounter unfolded, a messenger came,
Jairus's daughter was gone, life's candle aflame,
"Only believe," Jesus' words did impart,
With hope as their guide, they'd follow his heart.

In Jairus's house, mourning held sway,
Jesus declared, "She sleeps," to dismay's dismay,
In an upper room's chamber, He took her by hand,
"Arise, little girl," He spoke, life's command.

The girl's eyes fluttered open, breath anew,
The Savior's touch resurrected what once withdrew,
News of the miracle spread far and wide,
A healing touch, life's shadow defied.

Meditation: Reflect on the power of Jesus' touch to bring restoration to both the body and spirit and contemplate the significance of faith in receiving God's miraculous intervention.

Eyes of Faith – *Matthew 9:27-31*

In Capernaum's streets, two blind men did plea,
"Son of David," they cried, their hearts full of glee,
Jesus, the Healer, passing by their way,
"Have mercy on us," they fervently did pray.

Their plea did not fall on deaf ears that day,
Jesus touched their eyes, darkness gave way,
"According to your faith," He softly said,
Their eyes were opened, light's path widespread.

"See now," Jesus warned, "that no one will know,"
But their joy was uncontained, their faces aglow,
But in their excitement, they spread the word,
A Savior who heals, whose miracles are heard.

Meditation: Consider the profound transformation that occurs when faith and divine intervention converge, leading to physical and spiritual restoration.

Words of Wonder – *Matthew 9:32-34*

In Galilee's midst, a mute man did stand,
Bound by silence, unable to command,
A demon's grip held his speech captive,
A life overshadowed, a fate he'd fight to outlive.

To Jesus he was brought, seeking release,
A Savior's touch, a soul's inner peace,
The demon was cast out, the mute set free,
His lips were unsealed, his voice soared with glee.

Amidst the marvel, the Pharisees sneered,
Accusing Jesus of dark deeds, they jeered,
But the crowd marveled at the wondrous scene,
A mute man speaking, a Savior's grace seen.

Meditation: This story captures the power of Jesus' healing touch and the contrast between the crowd's marvel and the Pharisees' continued skepticism. Reflect on the transformative impact of Jesus' actions and the role of faith in witnessing miracles that defy the norm.

The Veil of Familiarity – *Matthew 13:53-58*

In Nazareth's streets, a familiar face,
Jesus returned, a teacher of grace,
To the synagogue He came to teach,
Words of wisdom, truth to reach.

The townspeople whispered, surprised yet unsure,
"Isn't this the carpenter's son?" they implore,
They saw the child, not the man before them,
The Son of God, whose light would illumine.

Their doubt held sway, their hearts closed tight,
A prophet without honor in his own sight,
Miracles and wisdom they had heard,
But in their familiarity, faith was blurred.

Jesus marveled at their disbelief,
A prophet without honor, despite his relief,
He left them to their hardened hearts,
A lesson learned; a truth imparts.

Meditation: Here Jesus returns to Nazareth and encounters skepticism among his own townspeople. Think of how this poem delves into the theme of familiarity breeding disbelief and explores the concept of how preconceived notions can hinder one's ability to recognize profound truths. Reflect on how our own biases and familiarity can impact our perception of divine messages.

The Journey of Empowerment – *Luke 9:1-6*

With purpose and courage, they rose at His call,
Disciples went forth, surrendering all.
To preach the kingdom, its nearness to tell,
They walked paths unknown where faith would dwell.

Empowered with authority, they went,
Healing and casting out, their intent,
No staff, bag, or bread did they take,
Dependent on God's provision, a faith awakes.

In towns and villages, their message spread,
The kingdom's arrival, its truth widespread,
They shook off dust from places unkind,
A symbol of judgment left behind.

Their impact was felt, the sick were healed,
Good news proclaimed, the truth revealed,
A journey of empowerment, a trust embraced,
In God's hands, their steps interlaced.

Meditation: This poem highlights the disciples' empowered mission, their dependency on God's provision, and their role as bearers of healing and transformation. Contemplate the concept of divine empowerment and the courage needed to step out in faith to spread a message of hope and transformation.

A Tragic Tale of Conscience – Mark 6:14-29

In the palace's corridors, whispers did weave,
Of Jesus' name, miracles believed,
Herod's troubled heart, a conscience stirred,
A prophet's voice echoed; a message heard.

John the Baptist, imprisoned and bound,
Preached truth unyielding, a voice resounds,
Herod's intrigue held him, a curiosity keen,
A prophet's message, a kingdom unseen.

Herodias's daughter danced, a banquet's delight,
Herod's oath given, a plot took flight,
A gruesome request, a mother's demand,
John's life extinguished, in a plot's cruel hand.

A beheading, a prophet's fate sealed,
A tragic tale of conscience revealed,
Herod's remorse, a heart heavy with blame,
A prophet's voice silenced, a life's flame.

Meditation: This poem highlights the complex dynamics of power, intrigue, and conscience, centering around Herod's internal struggle as he grapples with his actions. It invites reflection on the consequences of decisions made under societal pressures and personal convictions, ultimately leading to a grim outcome.

A Feast of Abundance – *John 6:1-14*

Beside the sea's gentle lull, a multitude did gather,
Hungry hearts seeking, a purpose to tether,
Jesus, a shepherd of souls, his gaze aware,
A feast of compassion, a miracle to share.

Five thousand gathered, a hungry throng,
In the wilderness's expanse, they longed for long,
A boy's meager offering, five loaves, two fish,
In Jesus' hands multiplied, a lavish dish.

Jesus gave thanks, his hands blessed the bread,
The fish, a symbol of life, multiplied, it spread,
The multitude ate, their hunger's hold abated,
A feast of abundance, a hunger sated.

Twelve baskets of fragments, a miracle's excess,
In scarcity's presence, divine generosity impressed,
A lesson in provision, faith's testament bold,
A feast of grace, a story to be told.

Meditation: This poem emphasizes Jesus' compassion, his ability to provide abundantly even in times of scarcity, and the lasting impact of faith in his miracles. It invites reflection on the significance of sharing, trust in divine provision, and the transformative power of a simple act of generosity.

Walking on Water – *John 6:15-21*

Beside the darkened sea, a tale of wonder unfurled,
A storm-tossed boat, a fearful world,
Jesus, a beacon of hope, on water's crest,
A miracle awaited, nature's test.

His disciples rowed, the winds against,
In darkness's embrace, their fears commence,
Then a figure approached, a sight surreal,
Jesus walking on water, their doubts to heal.

"Take heart, it is I," his voice they heard,
Fear transformed to wonder, faith stirred,
Peter, impulsive, stepped onto the wave,
For a moment, water's surface he'd brave.

But doubt crept in, his focus waned,
Sinking he cried, a plea unfeigned,
Jesus reached out, his hand extended,
Rescuing Peter, fear suspended.

The storm's fury ceased, the boat reached land,
A lesson in faith, a miraculous hand,
Walking on water, a testament profound,
In Jesus' presence, life's storms unbound.

Meditation: This story highlights the disciples' fear and doubt which become transformed into wonder and faith through the power of Christ. Contemplate the themes of trust, the miracles that challenge our understanding, and the calm that comes when we place our faith in the Divine presence amidst life's storms.

The Gentle Touch – *Mark 6:53-56*

On the shore they arrived, a journey complete,
Gennesaret's land, a place of retreat,
Jesus' fame spread like wildfire's blaze,
A healer's touch, a crowd's amazed gaze.

Boat's bow kissed the sand, disciples stepped down,
News of his coming spread through the town,
Sick on mats, ailing and frail,
Desperate for healing, stories of travail.

The news spread wide, a flame reawoke,
To Jesus they came through dust and smoke.
"Even his garment," the hopeful had taught,
Could carry the grace that silver bought not.

A woman approached, her faith ablaze,
Through the crowd she pressed, a hand to graze,
A touch of his robe, a touch of his might,
Years of suffering surrendered to light.

Her flow of blood ceased, her ailment no more,
In an instant, healing's tide did pour,
Amazed she stood, her heart full of praise,
A moment with Jesus, her life's turning phase.

The crowd pressed on, through every street,
Laying the sick, at Jesus' feet,
All who touched Him were made whole,
A healing touch, a redemption's goal.

Meditation: Reflect on the power of faith, the transformative nature of Christ's touch, and the idea that a simple encounter with the Divine can lead to profound healing and wholeness.

The Matters of the Heart – *Matthew 15:1-20*

Pharisees and scribes, self-righteous in stance,
Confronting the Lord with their critique askance,
"Why do your disciples transgress tradition's hold?
For they eat with unwashed hands, we're told."

Jesus, perceiving their hearts' hypocrisy,
Addressed their concern with words so free,
"Around rules of men, you've built your case,
Neglecting the heart, true purity's grace."

Isaiah's prophecy He quoted with might,
Their worship in vain, their hearts far from right,
With traditions they honored, their lips praised high,
Yet hearts held captive, far from the sky.

He summoned the crowd, his voice to unfurl,
"Listen and understand," He did whirl,
It's not what goes in that defiles the soul,
But what comes from the heart, the inner's role.

Evil thoughts, murder, adultery's stain,
Deceit, greed, hypocrisy's bane,
All from within arise and defile,
Matters of the heart, like venom, beguile.

As He spoke, the crowd was in awe,

A paradigm shift, a truth to draw,

It's the heart's transformation, the inside's grace,

That defines a soul, that sets its pace.

Meditation: Here Jesus confronts the Pharisees about their focus on external rules rather than the state of their hearts. Contemplate the nature of true purity, the significance of inner transformation, and the importance of aligning one's heart with their outward actions.

THE BREAD OF ABUNDANCE – *MARK 8:1-9*

In a desolate place, a multitude amassed,
Hungry hearts seeking, a moment unsurpassed,
Three days they'd followed, hunger pangs a plight,
Jesus' compassion stirred, a feast to ignite.

Seven loaves, a few fish, meager supply,
Yet with faith, the multitude they'd satisfy,
Jesus took the loaves, looked up to the skies,
Blessed and broke, with love in his eyes.

Distributing to disciples, hands to impart,
They shared with the crowd, a gift from the heart,
The feast began, a miracle's embrace,
Abundance from scarcity, a divine trace.

Four thousand were filled, a multitude's cheer,
Satisfied hearts, a moment held dear,
Seven baskets of leftovers, blessings untold,
From a humble beginning, a story unfolds.

A lesson emerged, a truth to unveil,
Jesus' provision, love's sail,
In scarcity, He brings abundance untold,
The Bread of Life, a story to be retold.

Meditation: Reflect on Jesus' provision, his ability to transform scarcity into abundance, and the spiritual nourishment He offers as the Bread of Life.

SEEKING SIGNS – MARK 8:10-13

Amidst miracles, a murmuring crowd,
Pharisees and skeptics, voices loud,
Seeking a sign, doubting hearts entwined,
In quest of proof, truth's light maligned.

Jesus sighed deep, a weary breath,
Their hardened hearts, a cause of death,
"No sign shall be given," He spoke clear,
Except for Jonah's tale, a truth sincere.

As Jonah emerged from the belly's hold,
Three days and nights, as the tale is told,
So the Son of Man, in death's domain,
Would rise victorious, eternal reign.

A lesson to heed, a message profound,
Signs won't suffice, faith must be found,
In Christ's resurrection, the ultimate sign,
A promise fulfilled, divine design.

Meditation: This story emphasizes the significance of Jesus' upcoming resurrection as the ultimate sign of his identity and mission. Reflect upon the role of faith and the profound nature of Christ's resurrection as the cornerstone of belief.

Yeast of the Pharisees – *Matthew 16:5-12*

Amidst the whispers of a weary land,
Jesus and his disciples, a faithful band,
A warning sounded, a lesson to impart,
Against the yeast of Pharisees, a caution from the heart.

"Beware," He urged, their leavened ways,
Their hypocritical façade, a truth ablaze,
Their teachings tainted, their hearts impure,
A call to discern, a warning to ensure.

The disciples puzzled, their minds perplexed,
Concerned for bread, their thoughts intermixed,
Jesus clarified, his message unveiled,
Not about bread, but falsehoods detailed.

Remember the miracles, the loaves, and fish,
Trust in God's provision, a faithful wish,
In spiritual matters, beware the leaven's strife,
Hold steadfast to truth, the abundant life.

Meditation: Within this poem we see the importance of discernment and the need to guard against the influence of hypocrisy and false teachings. Reflect on the contrast between external appearances and genuine faith, urging believers to focus on the essence of truth and trust in God's provision.

The Test of Allegiance – *John 6:67-71*

In the wake of miracles, a crowd's stirring,
Jesus' teachings, minds considering,
Disciples faced a moment of choice,
A test of allegiance, a still, small voice.

"Will you also go away?" He questioned deep,
A challenge to the hearts that steep,
Simon Peter, with conviction replied,
"Lord, to whom shall we go?" he voiced inside.

Words of life and truth, from Christ they came,
Eternal realities, beyond worldly acclaim,
Judas, a stark contrast, a heart concealed,
A traitor's seed, his loyalty revealed.

Yet among the Twelve, a bond remained,
A glimpse of faithfulness, a legacy ingrained,
In loyalty and surrender, the path was clear,
Following the Messiah, with hope sincere.

Meditation: This poem examines the contrast between Peter's resolute faith and Judas' eventual betrayal. Reflect on the nature of true discipleship, the challenges of allegiance, and the significance of staying devoted to the teachings of Christ despite difficulties.

The Cost of Discipleship – *Luke 9:22-25*

Amidst the disciples, a pivotal hour,
Jesus spoke of suffering, a path to empower,
He foretold his death, a mission profound,
A sacrifice destined; love's grace unbound.

"The Son of Man must suffer," He proclaimed,
A destiny heavy, a purpose unblamed,
Rejected by leaders, scorned by the wise,
In humility's embrace, salvation would rise.

Denying oneself, a cross to bear,
Losing life for Christ, a call to share,
For earthly gain, what price could suffice,
When one forfeits soul, the cost is the prize.

Yet in these verses, hope's flame would ignite,
Resurrection's promise, a dawn beyond night,
For through the suffering, the cross, the pain,
Eternal redemption, life's loss is the gain.

Meditation: Here is emphasized the theme of self-sacrifice and the profound transformation that comes from embracing Christ's call, even in the face of suffering. Contemplate the eternal perspective and the cost of true discipleship.

Transfiguration's Glimpse – *Mark 9:1*

On a mountaintop's crest, a moment divine,
Jesus transfigured, his radiance would shine,
His clothes turned dazzling white, a glimpse of his might,
A foretaste of glory, a celestial light.

Peter, James, and John, their eyes opened wide,
Beheld Moses and Elijah, side by side,
Conversing with Jesus, a sacred encounter,
Prophets of old, a moment to ponder.

A cloud descended, God's voice did declare,
"This is my beloved Son, my joy beyond compare,"
Listen to Him, the Father's command,
A declaration of purpose, a divine plan.

In Transfiguration's glory, a vision so grand,
A glimpse of the future, God's sovereign hand,
The disciples amazed, their hearts full of awe,
In this moment of revelation, the divine law.

Meditation: This is a truly awe-inspiring moment, the presence of Moses and Elijah and God's affirmation of Jesus as his Son. Reflect on the divine revelation and the transformative power of encountering Christ's glory.

The Veil of Understanding — *Luke 9:43-45*

Amid marvels, wonders untold,
Jesus foretells his suffering, a story to unfold,
Amidst the crowds' admiration, the disciples' pride,
A shadow of future trials, he'd confide.

The people amazed, yet mysteries lay,
Jesus' path ahead, a somber display,
He tells of betrayal, of pain and of loss,
A message of suffering, carried like a cross.

But the disciples, veiled by their own desire,
Could not fathom his words, their hearts on fire,
A curtain of unknowing, a barrier to see,
The depth of Christ's journey, his destiny.

Yet during confusion, a seed of hope,
The Resurrection's promise, a divine scope,
For beyond the suffering, the veil would be torn,
A victory triumphant, on Easter morn.

Meditation: We can sympathize with the disciples struggle to grasp Jesus' message in this poem. It also hints at the greater hope that lies beyond the veil of suffering. Reflect on this balance between suffering and hope in the context of Jesus' journey.

The Coin of Divine Provision – *Matt. 17:24-27*

In Capernaum's midst, a question arose,
Tax collectors questioned, the temple's dues imposed,
A coin of tribute, a symbol of might,
A worldly demand, a spiritual insight.

Peter approached Jesus, his voice sincere,
Concern for the payment, a matter quite clear,
"Doesn't the king's family pay, you see?"
Jesus' response held a lesson to be.

A fish in the sea, a treasure untold,
A coin in its mouth, a miracle to behold,
A demonstration of divine provision's sway,
In every challenge, a way made each day.

The coin retrieved, the tribute paid,
A lesson of faith in the words displayed,
In God's kingdom, the earth, and its stores,
Resources abundant, behind unseen doors.

Meditation: Tax season can be very stressful and here we see Jesus providing a miraculous solution on how to pay the temple tax. Reflect on how faith and trust in God can lead to unexpected blessings and solutions, even in challenging situations.

Lessons in Humility & Salt – Mark 9:33-50

Amidst the disciples, a question did stir,
Debating greatness, a concern that would blur,
"Who's the greatest?" they pondered, their hearts revealed,
Jesus' response, a truth unconcealed.

A child He brought forth, a symbol of grace,
In innocence and trust, a lesson took place,
"Receive the little ones," Jesus declared,
Humility's value, a virtue compared.

Infirmities addressed, temptations abhorred,
A call to cut off what causes discord,
A teaching on salt, a flavor to share,
Preserving righteousness, in love's tender care.

Salt's savor preserved, disciples must be,
Shining like lights, for all eyes to see,
A warning of stumbling, a plea to be true,
In humility and saltiness, faith to renew.

Meditation: This poem emphasizes the value of humility and integrity in one's actions and encourages readers to reflect on their roles as ambassadors of faith and love.

Divine Timing – *John 7:2-9*

In Judea's region, a festival near,
Jesus' brothers urged, with intentions clear,
"Show yourself openly, your followers to see,"
Misunderstanding his purpose, a plan not to be.

The world's time wasn't his, a truth understood,
Not revealing Himself, though intentions were good,
He remained in Galilee, a purpose divine,
Divine timing in play, a plan so sublime.

The world couldn't hate them, his brothers in view,
But his message they'd grasp, in time's avenue,
A journey unfolding, truths yet to unfold,
Divine mysteries waiting, stories yet to be told.

Meditation: There is a significance of divine timing and the misunderstandings that can arise when human plans clash with God's purpose. Jesus' brothers urge Him to reveal Himself openly but Jesus chose to remain in Galilee to continue his work. Reflect on how we need to trust God's timing and seek deeper understanding in the unfolding of divine mysteries.

Seeking Wisdom – *Matthew 19:1*

Amidst the changing winds of time,
A crowd gathers, seeking the sublime,
To Jesus they come, hearts laid bare,
In search of wisdom, burdens to share.

Amidst the tales of ancient lore,
The crowds assemble on the shore,
In this moment, a question's seed,
A test of wisdom, a soul's need.

"Is it lawful to divorce?" they ask,
A query deep, a pondering task,
With words deliberate, Jesus replies,
From God's intention, love never lies.

In this interaction, truth unfurled,
A lesson to ponder, for each heart to swirl,
A dialogue of faith, compassion's plea,
In Matthew's pages, wisdom's decree.

Meditation: Reflect on the timeless quest for wisdom and the human desire to find guidance in moments of moral uncertainty. Just as the crowd approached Jesus with their concerns, we too seek guidance in navigating life's complexities.

Chapter 5: The Celestial Journey

This chapter concerns Jesus' Southern Ministry which further unveiled his divinity and purpose. As He ventured into the southern territories, He continued to proclaim his message of love, forgiveness, and redemption. The teachings He shared carried a universal resonance, transcending societal boundaries and connecting with people from all walks of life. His words penetrated deeply as He addressed spiritual truths, ethical conduct, and the inner workings of the human heart. This ministry period exemplifies Jesus' commitment to the holistic transformation of individuals and society, showcasing his role as a spiritual guide and moral exemplar.

Miraculous events featured prominently in Jesus' Southern Ministry, emphasizing his divine authority and compassionate nature.

The healing of the sick, the restoration of sight, and the casting out of demons not only showcased his power over physical and spiritual afflictions but also symbolized his mission to bring wholeness to broken lives. These miracles served as tangible manifestations of his role as the promised Messiah, fulfilling prophecies and drawing people closer to understanding his identity.

Jesus engaged in deep interactions with individuals that transcended societal norms and cultural barriers. His encounters with outcasts, sinners, and marginalized individuals demonstrated his unconventional love an inclusivity. These interactions highlighted Jesus' unwavering commitment to reaching every soul, regardless of their background or past, affirming his role as the Savior of all humanity.

The Southern Ministry period also marked significant confrontations with religious authorities and challenges to his message. Jesus' debates and discussions with scholars and Pharisees revealed his profound knowledge of the Scriptures and his ability to penetrate the heart of religious matters. His teachings continued to expose the contrast between genuine faith and empty rituals, inviting individuals to embrace a deeper relationship with God.

Join me as we embark on a transformative journey through the Southern Ministry of Jesus through a series of evocative poems which illuminate his profound teachings, miraculous deeds, and empowering encounters. Let these poems be your guide, inviting you to delve deep into the heart of Jesus' mission and discover the timeless relevance of his ministry in today's world.

Whispers of Faith and Doubt – John 7:2-53

Amidst the bustling city's crowded street,
A whisper of anticipation, hearts to meet,
Jerusalem's feast, a gathering of many,
Intrigue and questions, a longing so uncanny.

Jesus, the center of both doubt and praise,
A figure of mystery, in myriad ways,
Whispers in the crowd, debates arise,
Is He the Messiah? Truth in disguise?

A feast of Tabernacles, a time of reflection,
Jesus' words stir hearts, a divine connection,
"My teaching is not mine, but His who sent me,"
A message of truth, hearts eager to see.

Divisions in the crowd, opinions varied,
Some scoffed and doubted, others were carried,
By the wisdom that flowed from Jesus' lips,
A truth that resonates, a journey that equips.

As days passed on, the tension grew,
Religious leaders questioned, skepticism they drew,
Yet amid doubt, faith took root,
Some recognized the truth, a life's pursuit.

During conflict, Jesus stood strong,
A beacon of hope, teaching all along,
His words and presence, a challenge to see,
The divine truth, a call to be free.

In Jerusalem's midst, a tale did unfold,
Of faith and doubt, of stories untold,
Through this chapter's verses, we find our place,
In the dance of belief, in God's endless grace.

Meditation: Explore your beliefs and doubts in the journey of faith. Think about the contrasts between those who doubted and those who recognized the truth. This serves as a reminder that faith is often a personal choice, rooted in a willingness to open our hearts to divine wisdom.

Mercy's Embrace – *John 8:1-11*

In the temple's court, a scene unveiled,
A woman caught in sin, her fate impaled,
The Pharisees gathered, judgment in hand,
Seeking to accuse, to condemn, to demand.

They present their case, her guilt proclaimed,
The law as their weapon, her soul to be maimed,
Yet Jesus appears, a voice of calm,
Writing on the ground, a healing balm.

He challenges them, those without sin to throw,
The first stone of justice, to let judgment flow,
Silence ensues, conviction takes hold,
From oldest to youngest, the stones they withhold.

One by one, they depart from the scene,
Leaving the woman alone, her heart now serene,
Jesus asks, "Where are your accusers, dear?"
"No one condemns you? Then neither do I, here."

Mercy's embrace envelops her form,
Her life spared from darkness, from storm,
"Go and sin no more," Jesus imparts,
A second chance granted, a fresh start.

Meditation: Through the contrast between the Pharisees' condemnation and Jesus' merciful response, this poem highlights the profound impact of Christ's compassion and the call to a life of renewed purpose and righteousness. Contemplate the themes of judgement, forgiveness, and the transformative power of grace.

Light of the World – *John 8:12-20*

In the temple's courts, a setting profound,
Jesus stands, his voice resounds,
"I am the light of the world," He proclaims,
A beacon of truth, dispelling doubts' claims.

Pharisees challenge, their skepticism displayed,
"You bear witness of yourself," they've conveyed,
Jesus responds, his testimony clear,
"My witness is true, my Father is near."

He speaks of departure, his heavenly origin,
Their lack of understanding, a spiritual chagrin,
He warns of their fate, without his embrace,
Lost in darkness, devoid of grace.

The Pharisees question, seeking to confound,
Jesus remains steadfast, his mission unbound,
"I am from above," He declares with might,
A truth to enlighten, to set hearts alight.

Meditation: This poem invites contemplation on the themes of spiritual illumination, divine origin, and the contrast between light and darkness. Through Jesus' declaration, the poem underscores his role as the source of truth and guidance in a world fraught with confusion and doubt. Think on this as you observe the interaction with the Pharisees and the tension between human skepticism and the profound nature of Christ's teachings.

Freedom's Call – John 8:21-59

In the temple's chambers, a discourse unfolds,
Jesus speaks of truth, a story to be told,
He foretells his departure, a mystery vast,
Pharisees question, doubting the forecast.

"I am from above," He boldly proclaimed,
His heavenly truth by few hearts acclaimed.
He pierced through doubt, their hardened stance,
Yet offered them grace—a second chance.

He proclaims, "You shall know the truth,"
And the truth shall set you free, uncouth,
Pharisees balk, descendants they claim,
But bondage persists, a spiritual flame.

The Father's honor, Jesus seeks to maintain,
A unity with God, a purpose to explain,
Pharisees argue, a lineage upheld,
But Jesus speaks of Abraham, a tale compelled.

He declares, "Before Abraham was, I AM,"
Divine identity, a truth to cram,
Pharisees take offense, stones they clutch,
Jesus hides, their intentions He would not touch.

Meditation: Through his teachings, Jesus challenges the Pharisees' misguided reliance on their heritage and emphasizes the need for true spiritual understanding and freedom. Consider the themes of spiritual liberation, Jesus' identity as the 'I AM,' and the tension between human pride and divine truth.

The Light of Sight – *John 9:1-41*

In a world of darkness, a man blind from birth,
A canvas of shadows, a life without mirth,
Jesus approaches, disciples inquire,
The cause of blindness, a truth to inspire.

Jesus responds, "Neither sin nor birth's role,
But for God's work, his purpose to extol,"
He spits, forms clay, applies to the eyes,
Bids the man to wash, to his surprise.

The blind man obeys, eyes open wide,
A world of colors, light's grace applied,
A miracle witnessed, a healing profound,
Yet skepticism abounds, voices resound.

Pharisees inquire, doubting the sight,
A Sabbath healing, a truth to ignite,
They question the man, his tale they dissect,
A battle of beliefs, a truth to protect.

The blind man testifies, his sight's newfound,
A prophet, he says, truth unbound,
The Pharisees scoff, reject his sight,
His blindness transformed, a journey's light.

Jesus confronts them, spiritual blindness He notes,
Pharisees claim sight, yet their hearts He denotes,
Blindness remains, not of the eyes,
A challenge to see, the heart's own ties.

Meditation: Reflect on the themes of physical and spiritual sight, the transformative power of Jesus' healing, and the contrast between true vision and the blindness of heart.

The Shepherd's Call – *John 10:1-21*

In pastoral scenes, a metaphor takes hold,
Jesus, the Shepherd, stories of old,
A gate, a flock, a voice distinct,
A parable's lesson, truth to depict.

The Shepherd enters, the gate's rightful door,
Sheep recognize his voice, they adore,
He leads them out to pastures wide,
Guides them with care, by his side.

Strangers' voices, the sheep won't heed,
They follow the Shepherd, a faithful creed,
A thief, a robber, seeks to steal,
But the Shepherd's protection, they feel.

Jesus declares, "I am the gate,
Through me, salvation's fate,
Enter through me, find pasture true,
Abundant life, I offer to you."

The Shepherd's love, a sacrifice known,
Lays down his life, his flock to atone,
A Good Shepherd, who knows each sheep,
In unity, their souls he'll keep.

Meditation: The parable emphasizes the importance of recognizing Jesus' voice, following his guidance, and finding spiritual safety and abundance in Him. The Shepherd's self-sacrifice and commitment to his flock underscore his love and devotion, as well as his invitation to abundant and eternal life through a relationship with Him. Reflect on Jesus' nurturing, guiding, and protective love for his followers, drawing parallels between the Shepherd's care for his sheep and Jesus' care for his people.

Sent as Laborers – *Luke 10:1-24*

A mission assigned, laborers sent forth,
Seventy disciples, a message of great worth,
Into towns and villages, they'd tread,
To prepare the way, as Jesus led.

The harvest ripe, workers few,
Jesus' command, a task to pursue,
He sent them as lambs amidst the wolves,
With no purse, no bag, no worldly tools.

A greeting of peace, a house to find,
A dwelling that's welcoming, hearts aligned,
Heal the sick, spread the word,
The Kingdom's near, its message heard.

Yet some won't listen, doors may close,
Dust from feet, a testimony shows,
Sodom's fate, a warning near,
Unrepentant cities, judgment's clear.

Returning disciples, joyous proclaim,
Even demons submit, in Jesus' name,
Their names in heaven, written bright,
Rejoice in Spirit's truth and light.

Meditation: The passage emphasizes the urgency of the mission, the importance of reliance on God's provision, and the power of Christ's name to overcome darkness and bring transformation. Despite challenges and rejection, the disciples return with joyful reports of their experiences, reminding us of the impact of sharing the Kingdom's message and the assurance of our names being written in heaven through our faith in Christ. Reflect on the disciples' role as laborers in the spiritual harvest, echoing Jesus' call to share the good news and extend his love and healing to all.

The Good Samaritan – *Luke 10:25-37*

Inquiring hearts, a teacher's inquiry,
A lawyer seeks, a truth to see,
"Who's my neighbor?" he asks to know,
A question to explore, a lesson to bestow.

Jesus responds, a parable takes shape,
A traveler beaten, left in a dire scrape,
A priest and Levite, passing by,
Ignoring his plight, their compassion awry.

Yet a Samaritan, a cultural divide,
Extends a hand, love's choice to confide,
Boundless compassion, wounds to mend,
His care knows no bounds, his aid he'll extend.

He binds his wounds, brings him to an inn,
Provides for his needs, paying every din,
A selfless act, a neighbor's heart,
Compassion's essence, a love to impart.

Jesus then asks, "Which was the true neighbor?"
The lawyer responds, truth's light to savor,
"The one who showed mercy," he declares,
A lesson learned, a heart that cares.

Meditation: The parable transcends cultural boundaries, emphasizing the universal call to love one's neighbor and to show mercy without hesitation. This story challenges us to examine our own attitudes and actions toward those in need, reminding us that true neighborliness goes beyond societal divides and expectations. The Good Samaritan exemplifies the kind of love and compassion that Christ calls us to exhibit in our daily lives, teaching us to recognize opportunities for kindness and to prioritize compassion over convenience. Reflect on the essence of true compassion, highlighting the contrast between the religious leaders' lack of action and the Samaritan's selfless care.

THE CHOICE OF MARY & MARTHA – *LUKE 10:38-42*

In Bethany's abode, a scene takes form,
Two sisters' choices, a lesson to inform,
Martha's bustling, a host's busy fret,
Mary's stillness, a moment to beget.

Martha serves diligently, a labor's grace,
Attending to details, a smile on her face,
Yet the tasks overwhelm, her frustration shown,
As she tends to the work, the dinner to own.

Mary, however, sits at Jesus' feet,
Absorbed in his words, in learnings sweet,
Martha complains, a plea for aid,
"Lord, tell her to help," her stress displayed.

Jesus responds gently, his words a balm,
"Martha, you're anxious, in needless qualm,
Mary's chosen the better part, you see,
To listen and learn, to be close to me."

A lesson unfolds, a contrast in view,
Between service's call and devotion true,
Both valuable choices, a balance to find,
In tasks and stillness, in heart and in mind.

Meditation: Through this story, Jesus teaches us about the importance of finding a balance between our responsibilities and our spiritual life. While service and action are significant, they must be accompanied by moments of stillness and devotion. Mary's choice to sit at Jesus' feet represents a desire for deeper connection and learning, highlighting the value of spending time in God's presence and nurturing our relationship with Him. Examine your own priorities and the need to strike a harmonious balance between your outward tasks and your inner spiritual growth. Reflect on the contrast between the sisters' choices: Martha's busy service and Mary's attentive listening.

Teach Us to Pray – *Luke 11:1-13*

In a quiet moment, disciples draw near,
A request they make, a prayer's atmosphere,
"Teach us to pray," they beseech the Lord,
To grasp the essence, to learn the Word.

Jesus responds, with a prayer to share,
The Lord's Prayer formed, a model of care,
"Our Father in heaven," the words begin,
A divine connection, a relationship to win.

"Hallowed be your name," reverence shown,
"Your kingdom come," a purpose to own,
"Give us this day," daily sustenance sought,
"Forgive our sins," a grace to be taught.

"Lead us not into temptation," a plea to guide,
"Deliver us from evil," in You we confide,
A prayer of unity, of dependence so pure,
A conversation with God, a pathway to endure.

Yet Jesus' teaching extends beyond words,
To persistence in prayer, faith that affords,
A parable shared, a friend's midnight call,
A plea for loaves, a lesson for all.

"Ask, seek, knock," Jesus imparts,
For the Father gives good gifts, in all hearts,
Just as a father responds to his child's plea,
So does God answer, abundantly free.

Meditation: Through this prayer, Jesus teaches us to approach God with reverence, to seek His kingdom and provision, to ask for forgiveness and guidance, and to acknowledge His power over temptation and evil. Additionally, the parable of the persistent friend underscores the value of consistent and persistent prayer, emphasizing God's willingness to respond to the sincere requests of His children. This narrative encourages us to cultivate a deeper prayer life, seeking a genuine connection with God and trusting in His goodness and generosity as we persistently ask, seek, and knock. Reflect on the significance of the Lord's Prayer as a model for connecting with God.

The Light & Darkness – *Luke 11:14-36*

Amid life's journey, a conflict unfolds,
A man possessed, darkness takes hold,
Blind and mute, trapped in despair,
Jesus brings deliverance, a love to repair.

The Pharisees, watching with skeptical eyes,
Accuse Jesus of using dark forces' lies,
But He counters their claims, with wisdom profound,
A divided kingdom crumbles, love knows no bound.

The Pharisees seek a sign from above,
A proof of His power, a sign of His love,
Jesus responds with a metaphor's grace,
A lamp's shining light, illuminating space.

The eye, a gateway to light and to dark,
Our choices, reflections, a transforming spark,
If the light within us is darkness concealed,
How great is that darkness, what truth is revealed?

The crowd's eager hearts, seeking truth's embrace,
They yearn for more, to see love's grace,
Jesus warns against hidden motives within,
Integrity's call, a heart free from sin.

Meditation: Through this metaphor, Jesus highlights the importance of the eye as a gateway to the soul, emphasizing the significance of the choices we make and the intentions of our hearts. He warns against hypocrisy and encourages us to pursue integrity and transparency. The narrative reminds us that Jesus is the ultimate source of light and truth, and by aligning our hearts with Him, we can dispel darkness and walk in the light of His love. Reflect on the power of Jesus' deliverance, His wisdom in addressing accusations, and His metaphor of the lamp.

WHITE SEPULCHERS – *LUKE 11:37-54*

Amidst Pharisees' scrutiny, a banquet unfolds,
Jesus dines with a purpose, truth to uphold,
A Pharisee's marvel at an unwashed hand,
Jesus responds with wisdom, a lesson to expand.

He points to their hypocrisy, a deeper intent,
Their focus on rituals, while hearts lay dormant,
Outward appearances, like whitewashed walls,
Hide inner corruption, truth's curtain falls.

Jesus' rebuke strikes, unmasking their guise,
"Whited sepulchers," a metaphor that implies,
The beauty outside conceals death within,
A heart without love, consumed by sin.

The lawyers too face Jesus' critique,
Burdening others, truth's message they tweak,
Suppressing God's wisdom, their hearts set askew,
A missed opportunity, love's call misconstrued.

In the face of opposition, Jesus stands strong,
His teachings challenging, exposing what's wrong,
He confronts hypocrisy with love's piercing gaze,
Urging us to seek truth and love's righteous ways.

Meditation:. The narrative encourages us to examine our own hearts and motives, recognizing the importance of integrity and genuine love. Jesus' courage in confronting religious leaders with the truth serves as a reminder to seek humility and authenticity in our faith journey. Through His words, He urges us to align our hearts with God's wisdom, focusing on love and righteousness rather than empty rituals. Reflect on the tension between outward appearances and inner authenticity. Jesus' metaphor of "whited sepulchers" serves as a powerful visual representation of the contrast between surface beauty and hidden corruption.

Fear Not, Little Flock – *Luke 12:1-59*

In a crowd's midst, a warning begins,
Jesus speaks caution, casting off sins,
Beware hypocrisy, secrets brought to light,
Fear God, not men, in truth's pure sight.

He offers comfort to disciples in the fray,
"Fear not, little flock," He tenderly conveys,
Trust in God's providence, a promise to unfold,
Treasures in heaven, a lasting gold.

A parable follows, a watchful master's tale,
Blessed are those found faithful, without fail,
Prepared for His return, vigilant in grace,
In readiness, they await His face.

Jesus' teaching continues, about divisions to face,
Acknowledging conflicts that won't leave a trace,
But His presence brings peace, a light that shines,
Guiding us through turmoil, His love defines.

He exhorts watchfulness, like a servant's role,
Eagerly awaiting the master's stroll,
Blessed are those ready, when He shall appear,
Faithful and ready, with hearts sincere.

Fear not, little flock, His words resound,
In a world of troubles, hope is found,
Seek His kingdom first, lay worries aside,
For God's provision, in Him we confide.

Meditation: The poem reflects on Jesus' teachings about fear, hypocrisy, and being watchful in our faith journey. The title, "Fear Not, Little Flock," reflects Jesus' reassuring message to His followers, encouraging them to trust in God's provision, seek His kingdom, and be ready for His return. It underscores the importance of staying watchful, faithful, and prepared for Christ's return, while also finding comfort in His promise to care for us. Reflect on the tensions between faith and fear, worldly concerns, and eternal priorities.

Reflection on Tragedy – *Luke 13:1-5*

Amid conversations, a somber tone,
Tragedy's specter, a question sown,
Pilate's actions, mingling blood with sacrifice,
Jesus addresses the hearts' dark vice.

"Do you think these Galileans were worse?" He inquires,
"Did their sins dictate such fatal fires?"
A cautionary tale, a call to reflect,
Repentance's urgency, a truth to perfect.

The tower fell hard—Siloam's mournful cry,
Lives were lost as loved ones asked why.
"Were they worse sinners?" the question He posed,
"Repent, lest your own fate be likewise closed."

"Unless you repent, you'll perish the same,"
A truth with eternal claim,
Looking beyond the tragedies of the day,
Repentance's importance, in life's array.

Meditation: The poem reflects on the human tendency to seek meaning in tragic events and Jesus' response by pointing to the need for repentance. The title highlights the themes of reflection, tragedy, and repentance. It emphasizes the importance of turning toward God in the face of both life's trials and the eternal perspective. Consider the significance of repentance as a response to life's uncertainties and as a reminder of our need for a transformed heart.

The Parable of the Fig Tree – *Luke 13:6-9*

A fig tree in a vineyard's soil,
A parable's tale, a lesson's coil,
For three years it bore no fruit,
A barren plight, a truth to compute.

The owner's patience, a waiting span,
He sought fruit, a harvest plan,
The vineyard keeper pled for time,
To cultivate, to prune, to climb.

"Let it alone for a year," he said,
"Let's nurture it, revive the dead,
Fertilize, water, give it care,
Perhaps it will bear fruit to share."

A fig tree's fate, a lesson to glean,
A call to change, to intervene,
In lives unfruitful, hearts grown stale,
A plea for transformation's trail.

Meditation: The title encapsulates the central theme of the parable, and the poem emphasizes the importance of nurturing and cultivating our lives to bring forth spiritual fruit. It speaks to the opportunities for growth and transformation, emphasizing the patience and care God extends to us as we journey toward a life marked by fruitful living. Delve into the symbolism of the fig tree as a representation of unfruitful lives and the call to bear spiritual fruit.

HEALED ON A SABBATH – *LUKE 13:10-17*

In the synagogue's sacred space,
A woman bound by a crippling trace,
For eighteen years, bent and bowed,
A life's weight, a soul enshrouded.

Jesus saw her, compassion's fire,
He called her forth, lifting her higher,
"Be set free from your ailment," He said,
His touch, a healing grace widespread.

The synagogue ruler's disapproving stare,
Indignant words, a Sabbath's affair,
"Six days for work, not healing day,
Why bend the rules?" he dared to say.

But Jesus' response, a rebuke clear,
"You hypocrites," his words severe,
Shouldn't this woman, a daughter of Abraham,
Be freed from her chains, healed in the Lamb?

He silenced the ruler with wisdom and grace,
Restored the bent woman to her rightful place.
A Sabbath of mercy, not burden or bound—
In Jesus' touch, true healing was found.

Meditation: The healing of the woman symbolizes the transformative power of Jesus' love and serves as a reminder of his authority to bring freedom from physical and spiritual burdens. Reflect on the deeper meaning of the Sabbath and the compassionate heart of Jesus, who challenges legalistic perspectives to bring healing and liberation.

The Seed & the Leaven – *Luke 13:18-21*

Amidst the fields, a parable unfurls,
A mustard seed, a treasure for the world,
Though tiny, a potential vast,
A kingdom's growth, unsurpassed.

A seed sown, a tree's reach wide,
Birds find shelter, in its branches they hide,
From small beginnings, great things arise,
A kingdom's mystery, under the skies.

Another tale, leaven's quiet might,
Hidden in dough, out of sight,
Yet it leavens the whole, transforms its core,
A kingdom's presence, forevermore.

Meditation: The poem delves into the significance of the mustard seed and the leaven, highlighting how these parables illustrate the profound impact of the kingdom of God from seemingly small beginnings. The mustard seed grows into a large tree that provides shelter for birds, symbolizing the inclusive nature of the kingdom. The leaven's hidden transformation of the dough represents the kingdom's permeating and transformative presence. Contemplate the depth of these parables and their implications for understanding the nature and growth of God's kingdom.

Returning to the Source – *John 10:40-42*

Across the Jordan, Jesus did go,
To where John first baptized, waters' flow,
A place of beginnings, a journey's start,
A return to the source, a soulful heart.

Many came to Him, a crowd anew,
Recalling John's witness, his words so true,
Miracles abound, belief took root,
In that sacred space, truth's pursuit.

Reflecting on the past, a connection deep,
A revival of memories, treasures to keep,
John's testimony echoed, faith stirred,
In returning to the source, truth's voice heard.

Meditation: The poem explores the significance of this event as a point of connection between Jesus, John's testimony, and the people who gather around Him. It highlights the importance of grounding one's faith in the source of truth and returning to the essence of spiritual journey. Reflect on the power of remembering and reconnecting with the foundations of your beliefs.

The Great Banquet's Call – *Luke 14:1-24*

Amidst Pharisees' watchful eyes,
Jesus entered, a banquet's surprise,
A man with dropsy, a healing touch,
In compassion's embrace, love's clutch.

Observing guests' self-righteous play,
A parable He shared, truth's ray,
A great banquet prepared, a feast grand,
Invitations sent, across the land.

Yet excuses arose, a heart's retreat,
Priorities misplaced, desires to meet,
One declined for fields, another for kin,
A wedding feast ignored, world's din.

Anger and urgency, a servant's task,
Invite the poor, the blind, those the world masks,
Empty seats filled, a feast prepared,
In humility's hall, love's table shared.

Meditation: The poem emphasizes the contrast between the self-righteousness of those who declined the initial invitations and the humility of those who ultimately attended. It invites readers to consider the nature of spiritual invitations, the openness of the heart, and the significance of prioritizing God's invitation above worldly distractions. Reflect on the banquet of God's grace and the inclusivity that characterizes his call to all.

The Price of Faith – *Luke 14:25-35*

Amidst the crowds, Jesus stood,
A challenging message, misunderstood,
"Whoever comes to me, yet does not hate,
Family and self, cannot be my mate."

His call rang out—a challenge profound,
To walk love's path where no chains are bound.
The price was high, the road was steep,
Yet grace was sown for those who'd reap.

Counting the cost, a tower's height,
Discipleship's path, a vigilant sight,
Not a hasty venture, a life to embrace,
Built on faith's foundation, God's grace.

A salty salt, a flavor divine,
Preserving the truth, the Gospel's sign,
Losing saltiness, a lesson learned,
Disciples' commitment, in Christ's love earned.

Meditation: The poem invites readers to consider the radical call of Christ to put Him above all else, even family and self, and to count the cost of discipleship. It emphasizes the need for genuine commitment and the preservation of the Gospel's essence. Reflect on the depth of your dedication to Christ and the enduring nature of discipleship's sacrifice.

Parables of Lost and Found – *Luke 15:1-32*

In gatherings of sinners, tax collectors, and more,
Jesus spoke parables, teachings to explore,
Lost sheep, a shepherd's love displayed,
The one found, the ninety-nine delayed.

A lost coin's search, a diligent quest,
Joy in discovery, an outcome blessed,
A prodigal son's tale, a father's grace,
Restored, forgiven, love's embrace.

Lost and found, a theme profound,
A glimpse of God's love, unbound,
The Shepherd's care, the Father's joy,
A message of redemption, sins destroyed.

Meditation: The poem invites readers to explore the profound love and compassion of God, portrayed through the parables. Reflect on your own experiences of being lost and found in the embrace of divine grace. Contemplate the lengths God goes to restore his children, emphasizing the joy of redemption and reconciliation.

OF STEWARDSHIP & RICHES – *LUKE 16:1-31*

A shrewd manager's tale, a lesson to convey,
A worldly wisdom, a steward's display,
Unrighteous wealth, a tool to use,
For kingdom's sake, a choice to fuse.

The parable of the rich man and Lazarus told,
Contrasts of life, destinies unfold,
A wealthy life, a beggar's plight,
Eternal truth, in heavenly light.

Stewardship's call, a lesson's essence,
Managing well, God's gracious presence,
Riches of heaven, treasures above,
A focus on eternity, a call to love.

Meditation: The poem invites readers to reflect on their own attitudes toward wealth and resources, considering how their choices align with God's values. Contemplate the eternal implications of stewardship and the significance of using earthly wealth to impact heavenly realities.

Faith, Forgiveness, & Service – *Luke 17:1-10*

In teachings of Jesus, wisdom is laid,
A call to forgiveness, a choice to evade,
Offenses will come, a truth to concede,
Forgiveness the path, as Christ's followers lead.

A mustard seed's size, faith's humble start,
A power immense, to move mountains apart,
Faith's steadfast stance, a heart's resolute hold,
In God's strength, miracles unfold.

Servanthood's essence, a humble decree,
No self-praise or pride, but humility,
A master's role, a servant's obey,
A life surrendered, along faith's way.

Meditation: The poem invites readers to consider their attitudes toward faith, their willingness to forgive, and their approach to serving others with humility. Reflect on the transformative power of faith, the freedom that comes with forgiveness, and the beauty of living a life dedicated to serving God and others.

Restored from the Dead – John 11:1-44

In Bethany's village, a tale of despair,
Lazarus lay ill, sickness' heavy air,
Sisters in anguish, a plea they'd confide,
"Lord, come quickly," their hearts open wide.

Jesus delayed, a purpose concealed,
Divine timing at play, his power revealed,
Four days in the tomb, death's grip took hold,
A miracle awaited, a story yet to be told.

"I am the resurrection," Jesus declared,
Life's conqueror, hope's banner shared,
"Believe, and you'll see God's glory unfold,"
Faith's invitation, a promise of old.

The stone rolled away, a voice that called,
"Lazarus, come forth," life's triumph enthralled,
Bound by graveclothes, life renewed he'd find,
A foretaste of Christ's resurrection, entwined.

Meditation: The poem evokes contemplation on the power of Christ to overcome death, the role of faith in witnessing miracles, and the promise of resurrection for believers. Ponder the significance of Christ's role as the source of eternal life, and embrace the hope and transformation found in Him.

Seeds of Decision – *John 11:45-54*

A miracle performed, Lazarus restored,
Witnesses astir, a crowd's voices soared,
Pharisees and leaders, their hearts stirred,
Fear of Jesus' influence, their concerns incurred.

Gathered in counsel, a decision they'd make,
Jesus' growing influence, a concern at stake,
Caiaphas spoke, prophecy unaware,
One life for the nation, a plan laid bare.

Yet unknowingly prophetic, his words resound,
A sacrifice for many, a Savior's path found,
From that day forward, their plot did unfurl,
Jesus' destiny sealed, his mission, a sacred swirl.

Meditation: The poem inspires reflection on the complexities of human reactions to divine intervention, the irony of Caiaphas's words in the grander narrative of salvation, and the unfolding of God's plan even through human decisions. Consider the role of faith, prophecy, and the broader implications of choices in the unfolding story of Jesus' ministry.

Healing at the Fringe – *Luke 17:11*

On the fringe of a village, a desperate plea,
Ten lepers stood, seeking mercy's decree,
"Jesus, Master, have mercy on us," they cried,
A plea for healing, their suffering implied.

"Go, show yourselves to priests," He commanded,
Their faith in his words, their bodies demanded,
As they journeyed forth, a miracle did transpire,
Cleansed of their ailment, hearts lifted higher.

One, a Samaritan, turned back to give praise,
Gratitude overflowing, his voice did raise,
Jesus' compassion revealed, not bound by race,
A healer of bodies and souls, in his embrace.

Meditation: The poem invites reflection on the power of faith, the significance of gratitude, and the transformative impact of Jesus' compassion. The Samaritan's response highlights the universal nature of Jesus' healing and the importance of recognizing God's work in our lives. Ponder the themes of inclusion, thankfulness, and the boundless reach of Jesus' love and healing touch.

Kingdom's Mystery Unveiled – *Luke 17:20-37*

Amidst questions of when and where,
The Pharisees queried with curious care,
"O Kingdom of God, when shall it appear?"
Jesus' response unveiled a truth so clear.

"The kingdom's not bound by earthly sight,
Not defined by place or temporal light,
It's within you," He said, hearts to inspire,
A mystery unfolding, a truth to acquire.

A time would come, like Noah's days of old,
When life continued, heedless, and bold,
Then the Son of Man would be revealed,
His kingdom's glory, unconcealed.

Two in the field, one taken, one left,
A cosmic shift, a destiny deft,
Two at the mill, a fate to divide,
A separation profound, none could hide.

As days of Lot, fire, and brimstone's rain,
Sudden and swift, no time to refrain,
Vigilance urged, in readiness stand,
For the Son of Man's return, grand.

Meditation: Through Jesus' words, the poem encourages introspection, reminding us of the importance of staying watchful and prepared for the return of the Son of Man. The imagery of Noah's days and the events of Lot emphasize the suddenness and inevitability of Christ's return, urging us to live with a sense of anticipation and readiness for the coming kingdom.

OF HUMILITY & PERSISTENCE – *LUKE 18:1-14*

In tales of prayer and heart's desire,
Two parables unfold, lessons to inspire,
A widow persistent, a judge unjust,
A lesson in prayer, in God we trust.

She sought justice, relentless plea,
Though the judge delayed, she'd not flee,
Her persistence prevailed, a message clear,
Pray without ceasing, cast away fear.

And then a tax collector, humble and low,
Approached the temple with heart in tow,
His prayer simple, his posture meek,
A plea for mercy, a soul to seek.

A Pharisee stood, pride in his prayer,
A litany of deeds, a self-righteous air,
But the tax collector, in humility's plea,
Found God's mercy, salvation's key.

Jesus proclaimed, the humble exalted,
The proud, by comparison, are halted,
Two lessons intertwined, wisdom's guide,
Prayer and humility, side by side

Meditation: The contrasting parable of the Pharisee and the tax collector illustrates the power of humility before God, emphasizing that true righteousness comes not from self-righteousness but from a humble heart. Reflect on your own approach to prayer and humility, and be encouraged to seek God with persistence and genuine humility.

Children & the Kingdom – Matt. 19:13-15

Amidst the crowd, little children drew near,
Seeking Jesus' touch, hearts pure and clear,
Disciples rebuked, their concerns voiced,
But Jesus embraced them, his love rejoiced.

"Let the children come," He gently proclaimed,
For such as these, the Kingdom is named,
In their innocence, faith does reside,
A lesson of trust, hearts open wide.

The Savior's arms, a refuge of grace,
He blessed the children, their spirits to embrace,
A reminder to all, simple and true,
To enter the Kingdom, hearts must renew.

In these brief moments, a lesson profound,
The Kingdom's secrets in children are found,
In faith and humility, love, and awe,
Jesus' embrace welcomes all without flaw.

Meditation: Through Jesus' compassionate gesture, this poem encourages readers to approach God with the innocence and trust of a child, recognizing the depth of love and grace that awaits in the Kingdom. Reflect on the significance of childlike faith and humility in the context of entering the Kingdom of God.

THE RICH RULER'S DILEMMA – MARK 10:17-31

A rich young ruler, seeking eternal life's key,
Kneeling before Jesus, his question set free,
"Good Teacher," he asked, earnest and keen,
"What must I do to inherit life's serene?"

Jesus met his gaze, love's wisdom in sight,
"Keep the commandments," He replied, words light,
Yet the ruler persisted, his heart's yearning strong,
"What more?" he asked, seeking where he belonged.

"Go, sell all you have, give to the poor," Jesus spoke,
"Then follow me, and treasures in heaven evoke."
The ruler's face fell, a struggle within,
For his great wealth held him in a worldly spin.

Jesus, with love, saw his inner strife,
The pull of possessions, the allure of life,
"Hard for the rich to enter God's reign,"
A lesson profound, a truth to explain.

The disciples bewildered, the lesson took hold,
How riches and Kingdom can clash and unfold,
"Who then can be saved?" they questioned in awe,
Jesus' response echoed, a divine call.

With God, all things possible, He imparted,
A truth for the seeking, the faithful-hearted,
In surrender and trust, God's love comes alive,
Riches in heaven, where hearts truly thrive.

Meditation: Through the ruler's dilemma and Jesus' teachings, examine your own attachments, understanding that true wealth lies in surrendering to God's call and finding treasures in heaven. This poem ultimately conveys the message of the Kingdom's values and the transformative power of faith and sacrifice.

The Generous Vineyard Owner – *Matt. 20:1-16*

In a vineyard's morning, laborers stood,
A master approached, his plan understood,
Hiring workers throughout the day's light,
A promise of wages, a sense of what's right.

Early risers to latecomers, they came,
Each with their hopes, each with a name,
A denarius offered, a fair wage agreed,
For a day's toil under the sun's bright heed.

Yet as hours passed, the master returned,
More workers enlisted, no one spurned,
To all, he'd give as each journeyed his way,
An equal denarius, no matter the sway.

The early birds grumbled, their brows in a frown,
"This is unfair," they muttered, their voices renown,
"We bore the heat, yet they've earned as we did."
But the master's response shattered their bid.

"Friend, I've done no wrong, it's my choice to pay,
The same wage to all, at the end of the day,
Am I not allowed to do as I please?
Is your eye envious, your heart ill at ease?"

In this parable told, a message so clear,
The Kingdom's grace, without favor or fear,
The first shall be last, the last shall be first,
God's mercy and love, to all, he'd immerse.

Meditation: Reflect on the concept of God's grace and the Kingdom's values, which can challenge human notions of fairness and merit. Through the parable, examine your own attitude toward comparison, envy, and God's boundless mercy. The poem ultimately conveys the message of God's inclusive love, where all are invited to partake in the abundance of his Kingdom, regardless of their past or perceived worthiness

The Foretelling of Suffering – Luke 18:31-34

Amidst disciples' shadows, Jesus led,
A path of destiny, a fate to be spread,
He spoke of suffering, of pain to bear,
A prophecy unveiled; a cross to wear.

To Jerusalem's streets, his journey bound,
Betrayed, condemned, by foes to be found,
Scribes and elders, their plots to unfurl,
A dark cloud gathering, a destiny swirl.

Rejected, condemned, by those He came to save,
A fate foretold, a path he'd brave,
Yet disciples bewildered, in doubt and fear,
His words unclear, his mission near.

"Behold, we're going to Jerusalem," He said,
To fulfill prophecy, for redemption he'd tread,
Suffering, rejection, a grave's embrace,
Yet on the third day, resurrection's grace.

Meditation: This poem explores the disciples' confusion and fear in the face of these prophecies. Ultimately, the poem conveys the message of Jesus' steadfast commitment to his mission, despite the hardships He knows lie ahead. Reflect on the significance of Jesus' sacrifice and his willingness to endure suffering for the sake of humanity's redemption, and contemplate your own responses to the call of discipleship and sacrifice.

The Servant's Call – Matthew 20:20-28

A mother's plea, both humble and bold,
To Jesus she came, her longing told.
"Grant my two sons great honor and sight—
One at Your left, the other Your right."

Jesus responded with love in His gaze,
"Can you drink from my cup, endure life's maze?
True greatness, my friends, is in servanthood's role,
A humble heart's essence, a servant's soul."

The disciples' unrest, a lesson to teach,
A kingdom's values, beyond earthly reach,
"To serve, not be served," Jesus proclaimed,
A message of humility, in hearts to be framed.

A ransom for many, His life he'd give,
A sacrificial love, for all to believe,
In servitude's embrace, a lesson clear,
A call to humility, to hold others dear.

Meditation: By illustrating the contrast between the world's understanding of power and Jesus' example of servanthood, this poem encourages a deeper reflection on the significance of living out the values of Christ's kingdom in our daily lives. Consider your own attitudes toward leadership and greatness, and ponder how you can prioritize acts of service and love.

Blind Bartimaeus – *Luke 18:35-43*

On Jericho's road, a blind man's plea,
Bartimaeus sat, in darkness he'd be,
A cry for mercy, a plea for sight,
"Son of David, have mercy, make me right!"

The crowd's hushing, his voice they'd disdain,
Yet louder he cried, his faith not in vain,
"Jesus, Son of David, have mercy on me!"
A plea of desperation, a longing to see.

Jesus stood still, His command made clear,
"Call him," He said, dispelling all fear,
Bartimaeus arose, his cloak cast aside,
Led to Jesus, hope in his stride.

"What do you want?" Jesus asked, sincere,
"Lord, let me see," Bartimaeus' voice clear,
"Your faith has healed you," Jesus proclaimed,
Instantly sighted, darkness reclaimed.

A moment of transformation, a life made new,
Bartimaeus' faith, a lesson to construe,
From blindness to sight, from despair to light,
In Jesus' touch, his world set right.

Meditation: Through the imagery of Bartimaeus' transition from darkness to light, this poem encourages readers to examine their own spiritual vision and the role of faith in encountering the Divine Healer. Reflect on Bartimaeus' persistent faith and his boldness in seeking Jesus' mercy despite the crowd's disapproval. Contemplate the transformative power of encountering Jesus, both in physical healing and in the restoration of spiritual sight.

Zacchaeus' Redemption – *Luke 19:1-10*

In Jericho's streets, a tax collector's fame,
Zacchaeus by name, known for wealth's claim,
A man of small stature, a heart seeking more,
He longed to see Jesus, his heart to explore.

The crowd pressed in, a barrier he'd find,
So, he climbed a sycamore tree, a way to unwind,
Jesus passed by, His gaze upward cast,
"Zacchaeus, come down, for today we'll break fast."

Zacchaeus obeyed, his heart stirred within,
He welcomed the Savior, his life to begin,
A feast in his home, a transformation's start,
Jesus' presence warming, mending his heart.

The crowd murmured, judgment they'd profess,
For Zacchaeus' past, his life's brokenness,
"I give half my wealth," he declared with zeal,
"To the poor, restitution, my soul's appeal."

"Salvation has come to this house," Jesus declared,
A sinner redeemed, a life fully repaired,
Zacchaeus transformed, a tale to be told,
From seeking a glimpse to embracing love's hold.

Meditation: Through the imagery of a feast and the theme of salvation, this poem invites you to consider the profound impact of encountering Jesus' grace and the possibilities of personal renewal and reconciliation with God. It highlights Zacchaeus' boldness in seeking Jesus and his willingness to make amends for his past actions. Reflect on the power of encountering Jesus to change hearts and lives.

The Faithful Steward – *Luke 19:11-27*

A nobleman's journey, a distant terrain,
To receive a kingdom, his people to gain,
He entrusted his servants with talents, a task,
To steward his wealth, fulfill what was asked.

To one he gave five talents, a sum quite grand,
Another received two, in his hand,
And to the third, a single talent to hold,
Each steward's faith and diligence to unfold.

The first two worked diligently, increased what they had,
Doubled their talents, their efforts not clad,
But the third, fear's grip held him tight,
Buried his talent, hid it from sight.

The nobleman returned, his reckoning near,
The first two presented, success crystal clear,
"Well done, faithful servant," he voiced his acclaim,
"Enter into joy, share in my aim."

The third servant trembled, his talent retrieved,
Fearful of the nobleman's belief,
"Lazy servant," the nobleman replied,
Reaping no gain, letting fear reside.

The faithful stewards honored, entrusted anew,
The unfaithful, their role withdrew,
A parable's lesson, a truth to reflect,
Be faithful and diligent, God's will to detect.

Meditation: This poem contrasts the diligent efforts of the first two servants with the fear-driven inaction of the third. Through the narrative of the nobleman entrusting talents to his servants, the poem encourages you to reflect on your willingness to invest in God's kingdom and your faithfulness in using their gifts for His glory. It serves as a reminder to live with purpose and intentionality, embracing the call to be faithful stewards of what God has bestowed. Consider your own role as a steward of the resources and opportunities God has given you.

The Alabaster Offering – *John 11:55-John 12:1*

In Jerusalem's bustling streets, a Passover feast,
The people converged, anticipation increased,
Whispers of Jesus' arrival, a prophet revered,
Amidst the crowd's chatter, His message adhered.

Mary, Lazarus' sister, a heart moved by grace,
An alabaster flask, love's offering to embrace,
She entered the room, where Jesus reclined,
Her devotion poured out; a fragrance entwined.

With precious ointment, she anointed His feet,
Her tears mingling with ointment's scent sweet,
With her hair she wiped, love's act so profound,
A gesture of honor, in humility's bound.

Judas, indignant, questioned her intent,
"Why waste this ointment, for such sum it was meant?"
Jesus' response, a lesson to impart,
Her act of devotion, touched His very heart.

"The poor you'll always have, but not me always here,"
He praised her offering, wiped away her fear,
Her story told, a memorial's frame,
In gospel's pages, her love's eternal claim.

Meditation: This poem delves into the depth of Mary's love and her willingness to pour out her heart in an extravagant gesture of honor and worship. It contrasts her genuine act of devotion with Judas' critical response, emphasizing Jesus' affirmation of her actions. Through Mary's story, the poem highlights the beauty of selfless love and serves as an invitation to pour out our hearts in adoration and service to the Savior. Consider your own expressions of love and devotion to Christ, and reflect on the significance of sacrificial giving and humility before Him.

Witness of Lazarus – *John 12:9-11*

In Bethany's haven, a home warm and dear,
A dinner's aroma, a gathering near,
Lazarus, once dead, now living and whole,
A miracle's tale, a truth to extol.

The news spread like wildfire, a crowd amassed,
To see Lazarus living, a story unsurpassed,
Their curiosity piqued, their hearts filled with awe,
At the sight of one once trapped by death's jaw.

The Pharisees plotted, envy in their hearts,
A testimony strong, a threat to their parts,
Lazarus stood as a living testament,
A symbol of life's renewal, a grace so fervent.

Judas Iscariot's voice raised, cynicism spread,
"Why waste this ointment, for poor it could've fed?"
Yet Jesus defended the woman's choice,
Her offering of love, her heart's earnest voice.

Lazarus' presence, a witness profound,
A living proof of grace that abounds,
His story interwoven with Mary's gift,
A testimony to Jesus' power to uplift.

Meditation: This poem captures the intrigue and curiosity of the people as they gathered to see the man who had been raised from the dead. It also highlights the contrast between the Pharisees' envy and skepticism and Mary's sincere act of devotion. The title reflects Lazarus' role as a witness to the transformative power of Christ and the profound impact His resurrection had on those who witnessed it. Consider the significance of Lazarus' story as a testament to Jesus' authority and the hope of new life in Him. Reflect on the relationship between faith, miracles, and the response of the human heart.

Chapter 6: Crowned in Sacrifice, Resurrected in Glory

The upcoming chapter delves into the climactic moments of Jesus' Final Week on earth, including His crucifixion and resurrection. These events are at the very heart of the Christian faith, symbolizing Christ's ultimate sacrifice and triumph over sin and death. As we explore this significant period, the poems within this chapter will serve as a poignant guide, directing our attention to the core of Christ's eternal mission.

The crucifixion, a profound act of love and redemption, stands as a testament to Jesus' willingness to bear the weight of humanities sins. We will go on a harrowing journey together. His betrayal, brutal trial, and horrific death invites us to reflect on the magnitude of His sacrifice and depth of His love for us. Through vivid imagery and emotional resonance, these poems will help us enter the emotional and spiritual dimensions of the crucifixion, allowing us to connect with the profound significance of Christ's suffering.

Yet, the story does not end with the crucifixion; it culminates in the glorious resurrection, the triumph that marks the fulfillment of Christ's time on earth and the commencement for His eternal mission. The poems in this chapter will also guide us through the wonder and awe of this moment. Helping us truly understand the moments when Christ overcame death and opened the way into eternal life. I would encourage you to contemplate the power of God's grace and the hope that springs from the empty tomb.

Come now and share in the joy of the disciples who witnessed the risen Lord.

Triumphal Entry – John 12:12-19

Amidst the crowd's joyous song,
A triumphant entry, a throng strong,
Cloaks and branches strewn on the way,
Heralding Jesus, the King, that day.

Mounted on a humble colt, He rode,
The Promised One, in prophecy bestowed,
The Messiah's presence, hearts discern,
Hope and salvation, in Him to burn.

"Hosanna! Blessed is He who comes!"
A chorus rising, like heavenly drums,
Messiah embraced, palms waved high,
A moment of praise, the Savior nigh.

Yet beyond the jubilant cheer,
A deeper truth, a destiny clear,
This triumphant entry, a path decreed,
To a cross he'd go, for sin's deep need.

Meditation: Reflect on the paradoxical nature of this event— a triumphant welcome foreshadowing the ultimate sacrifice. Amidst the joyful celebration, the deeper significance of Jesus' mission is hinted at, as He takes the first steps towards the cross, offering redemption and eternal life.

The Cleansing of the Temple – *Matt. 21:10-19*

In the temple's sacred space, a scene unfolds,
Jesus enters with a purpose, His mission bold,
Merchants' tables overturned, coins scatter,
A cleansing fire, a divine matter.

"Is this not a house of prayer?" He proclaimed,
Zeal for God's house, a passion untamed,
The blind and the lame find healing's grace,
The temple transformed, a holy embrace.

Children's voices raised in praise,
"Hosanna to the Son of David," their refrain,
Religious leaders' hearts perturbed, they'd scheme,
But Jesus' work, a divine dream.

The fig tree withered, a lesson taught,
Faith's call, a spiritual thought,
A metaphor of bearing fruit so pure,
Faith's vitality, a foundation sure.

Meditation: Through the story of the fig tree, this poem encourages contemplation on the significance of faith and bearing spiritual fruit in our lives Reflect on Jesus' zeal for true worship and the transformative power of His presence.

The Hour of Glory – *John 12:20-50*

As Passover's feast approached with grace,
Greeks sought Jesus, seeking His embrace,
A voice from heaven, a declaration grand,
"The hour has come," a divine command.

A grain of wheat, in soil to die,
Life to spring forth, a truth to apply,
Jesus' imminent sacrifice revealed,
His love, His mission, His heart unsealed.

Yet many hearts were hardened still,
The light shone, but darkness's chill,
A choice to make, to walk in the light,
Or turn away, lost in night.

The words He spoke, eternal and true,
A judgment's scene, a life to review,
A Savior's call, a path to salvation,
His final week, a divine culmination.

Meditation:
This passage serves as a pivotal point in Jesus' ministry, and the poem encourages contemplation on the profound themes of salvation and judgment. Reflect on the significance of Jesus' impending sacrifice, His identity as the Light of the World, and the choice each person faces to accept or reject His message.

Authority & Parables – Mark 11:27-Mark 12:12

In the temple's courts, authority challenged,
Religious leaders questioned, their intent unbalanced,
By what right Jesus acted, His teachings proclaimed,
A dialogue of power, a truth to be named.

A parable woven, a vineyard's tale,
God's people unfaithful, their hearts set to fail,
Servants sent, but mistreated and scorned,
The landowner's son, by wickedness torn.

The cornerstone rejected, a symbol profound,
The Kingdom's truth, in parables found,
Religious leaders plotted, their envy concealed,
Yet Jesus' teachings, a mystery revealed.

Meditation: Contemplate the theme of authority, the rejection of the cornerstone, and the layers of meaning within the parable of the vineyard. Reflect on the significance of these teachings in the context of Jesus' final week and His eternal mission.

Cunning Questions – Luke 20:20-26

Amidst the shadows of intrigue and deceit,
Religious leaders conspired, a plot to complete,
A question designed, a trap to ensnare,
Their cunning attempts, Jesus' wisdom aware.

"Is it lawful to pay tribute to Caesar?" they posed,
Their intent clear, their motives exposed,
But Jesus, perceiving their treacherous aim,
Responded with wisdom, their snare to defame.

"Render unto Caesar," His answer so wise,
Yet beyond the coin's image, truth belies,
Render unto God, hearts, and souls true,
A message profound, for all to construe.

Meditation: Contemplate Jesus' wisdom in navigating the complexities of their inquiry and His ability to turn their intentions against them. The reflection on rendering unto Caesar and unto God underscores the spiritual dimensions of Jesus' teachings and His eternal mission.

Resurrection's Light – Mark 12:18-27

Skeptics and sages, a query they brought,
Of marriage and afterlife, a mystery sought,
They spoke of a woman, wed sevenfold,
"In the resurrection, whose wife will she hold?"

Jesus' response, a light to reveal,
Not limited by earthly bonds, a truth to unseal,
In realms divine, where angels abide,
Marriage is transformed, a heavenly guide.

Resurrection's dawn, a truth profound,
Beyond mortal ties, love's essence unbound,
For God of the living, a reality clear,
In eternal light, there's nothing to fear.

Meditation: Contemplate the nature of relationships beyond this earthly life and the transformative power of resurrection. Jesus' answer sheds light on the eternal dimension of love and life, redirecting focus from the temporal to the heavenly.

Love's Command – Matthew 22:34-40

Inquiry in earnest, a lawyer did pose,
A question of law, where love surely flows,
"Which commandment's greatest?" he inquired,
In a heart's pursuit, truth's essence desired.

Jesus' response, a call to embrace,
The heart of the law, in love's warm embrace,
"Love God with your all, heart, soul, and mind,
And love your neighbor, to all be kind."

Two commandments entwined, a foundation so true,
Love's essence revealed, in all that we do,
With heart, soul, and mind, and strength that we wield,
In love's radiant light, God's kingdom revealed.

Meditation: Meditate on the centrality of love in fulfilling God's will and building a harmonious community. By emphasizing these twin commandments, Jesus lays the groundwork for a life guided by love, rooted in God's unconditional and selfless affection.

Lord and Descendant – *Luke 20:41-44*

In the temple's sacred space, Jesus did stand,
A question He posed, minds to expand,
"Who is the Messiah? Tell me, do share,
Whose son, is he? Declare it clear."

"The son of David," they replied with might,
A descendant's claim, in the lineage's light,
But Jesus revealed a truth profound,
A mystery unfolding, faith's ground.

David's son, yes, but Lord as well,
In divine paradox, His story would swell,
From David's line, a Savior foreseen,
Both human and divine, God's plan pristine.

Meditation: Contemplate Jesus' unique identity and the intricate tapestry of His role as the fulfillment of Old Testament prophecies.

Beware the Hypocrisy – *Mark 12:38-40*

In the temple's solemn air, Jesus did observe,
Scribes and Pharisees, their status to preserve,
Robes flowing grand, places of honor they seek,
A facade of righteousness, the truth to tweak.

With long prayers and appearances grand,
Hypocrisy's grip tightened, like shifting sand,
Devouring widows' houses, a grievous wrong,
Religious acts a cover, integrity gone.

"Beware of such leaders," Jesus warned clear,
For their hearts were far from what they appear,
The hypocrites' destiny, a judgment near,
Their true intentions, the Lord brought clear.

Meditation: The poem serves as a cautionary tale against empty religiosity and underscores the significance of aligning our actions with our true beliefs. Reflect on the importance of sincerity and genuine faith, and Jesus' reminder to prioritize the state of our hearts over outward appearances.

The Widow's Offering – Mark 12:41-44

In the temple's bustling space, a widow stood,
With two small coins, her offering subdued,
Amidst the wealthy's clang, her offering fell,
A humble contribution, a tale to tell.

The rich gave much, their abundance on display,
But the widow's mites, in a different way,
She gave from her poverty, her heart's desire,
A sacrificial act, a faith that inspires.

Jesus noticed her quiet act of grace,
Her offering, small in the temple's vast space,
"Truly I tell you, "He proclaimed wise,
Her two coins outweighed, a truth to recognize.

Meditation: The poem emphasizes the principle of giving from a place of faith and willingness, regardless of the amount, and encourages us to cultivate a spirit of generosity that transcends mere appearances. Reflect on the nature of sacrificial giving, highlighting the value of a heart-felt offering over material abundance.

Signs of the Times – *Luke 21:5-36*

Amidst the temple's grandeur, disciples stood,
Marveling at stones, artistry imbued,
But Jesus foretold, a future unknown,
Not one stone standing, a truth to be shown.

"Take heed," He warned, signs of the times,
Deception and turmoil, as history climbs,
Nations in conflict, the earth's distress,
A world in turmoil, humanity's test.

Persecution would come, disciples to bear,
Yet wisdom and words, the Spirit would share,
A defense unyielding, a faith to proclaim,
In trials and hardships, believers' aim.

"Watch and pray," Jesus advised His own,
For His return, the signs would be shown,
In clouds of glory, His presence would shine,
Redemption's fulfillment, a promise divine.

Meditation: This poem encourages believers to remain steadfast in faith amidst the challenges of life, recognizing the signs that point to God's sovereignty over history and the ultimate restoration He promises. Reflect on the transient nature of worldly things, the importance of spiritual discernment, and the call to watch and pray in anticipation of Christ's ultimate fulfillment of redemption.

The Parable of Preparedness – Matt. 25:1-46

In midnight's hush, ten virgins await,
Five wise, five foolish, their lamps ornate,
The bridegroom's arrival, a moment unknown,
Preparedness urged, the truth to be shown.

The wise carried oil, their lamps burning bright,
Ready to meet him in the dead of night,
But the foolish unprepared, their lamps grew dim,
A lesson unfolded; their fate sealed within.

The parable of talents, another tale told,
Investments of faith, entrusted and bold,
Two servants multiplied, their master's delight,
One hid his talent, darkness took flight.

A final parable, the sheep, and the goats,
A separation foretold, redemption's coats,
Feed the hungry, clothe the poor,
The least of these, Christ's love to explore.

Meditation: The poem encourages readers to examine their own lives and choices considering these parables, emphasizing the eternal significance of our faith and deeds. Reflect on the importance of being spiritually prepared for Christ's return, using your God-given gifts wisely, and demonstrating Christ's love through compassionate actions towards others.

The Anointing of Jesus – *Mark 14:1-2*

In Bethany's humble abode, a moment of grace,
A woman with an alabaster jar, a fragrant embrace,
She approached the Savior, her heart's devotion,
A lavish anointing, a sacred emotion.

The jar held costly ointment, a treasure untold,
She poured it on Jesus, her love to unfold,
A gesture extravagant, a fragrant delight,
A demonstration of love, pure and bright.

Yet voices of criticism arose in the air,
"Why this waste?" they questioned, unaware,
But Jesus defended her, her act understood,
A preparation for burial, a story to be withstood.

Meditation: This poem encourages readers to consider the value of expressing their love for Jesus through generous and heartfelt acts, even when faced with misunderstanding or criticism. The anointing serves as a precursor to Jesus' impending sacrifice, deepening the significance of the moment. Reflect on the woman's act of extravagant love and devotion, as well as the contrasting reactions of those around her.

A Fragrant Offering – Matthew 26:6-13

In a house at Bethany, a scene unfolds,
A woman with a vial of perfume, stories untold,
She came to Jesus, her heart's devotion to convey,
A fragrant offering, a love that would stay.

The alabaster jar held costly nard,
She poured it on His head, a gesture to regard,
An act of worship, a scent that filled the air,
A moment of beauty, a moment rare.

But some voices protested, criticizing her deed,
"Why this waste?" they asked, sowing doubt and seed,
Yet Jesus saw beyond, He understood her heart,
Her act of love, her devotion, her sacred part.

He praised her for her deed, her act of grace,
For she anointed Him for His burial, a sacred embrace,
Her story remembered, her devotion renowned,
In the annals of history, her love's fragrance found.

Meditation: Jesus' recognition of the woman's act underscores the value of heartfelt devotion and the significance of preparing for important moments. The fragrance of her offering lingers as a testament to her genuine love and her understanding of Jesus' impending sacrifice. Reflect on the power of extravagant acts of love and worship, even when faced with criticism or misunderstanding from others.

BETRAYAL'S WHISPERS − *LUKE 22:3-6*

In the shadows of betrayal's embrace,
Judas, a disciple, veiled his true face,
A pact made in secret, a deal for gain,
Silver coins exchanged, a soul's stain.

Dark motives at play, greed's hold tight,
A heart deceived, veering from the light,
The adversary's whispers, doubts to sow,
Judas yielded, allowing treachery to grow.

He sought the chief priests, his plan unveiled,
To betray Jesus, a friend now derailed,
Thirty pieces of silver, the price agreed,
A plot set in motion; a faithful heart deceived.

Yet amidst the darkness, a lesson to find,
Judas' choices a warning for humankind,
A cautionary tale of how greed can blind,
And lead one astray from the divine.

Meditation: Judas' actions serve as a reminder of the vulnerability of the human heart to the lure of temptation and the importance of guarding against the influences that can lead us astray from our values and convictions. Reflect on the dangers of succumbing to greed and making choices driven by personal gain, even at the cost of betraying trust and friendship.

Preparation's Prelude – Luke 22:7-13

As Passover's feast drew near,
A room prepared, a moment clear,
Jesus instructed disciples, a task assigned,
To ready the place where they'd dine.

"Go into the city," Jesus spoke with grace,
"A man carrying water will meet your gaze,
Follow him, to his master's abode,
A place furnished, where we'll share this ode."

The disciples went forth, the plan revealed,
In a city of noise, where fate was sealed.
The upper room, with bread and wine,
Would host the start of love divine.

With unleavened bread and wine of the vine,
Symbolic of freedom, a divine design,
Jesus prepared to share His heart's song,
In a room appointed, where faith was strong.

Meditation: Reflect on the significance of preparation in our spiritual journeys. Just as Jesus gave specific instructions to His disciples, guiding them to the appointed place, we are reminded of the importance of heeding divine guidance and being attentive to the signs and opportunities that lead us to meaningful encounters with God.

Communion's Covenant – *Mark 14:17*

Around a table, hearts gathered near,
A solemn moment, anticipation clear,
Jesus and disciples, an intimate scene,
Sharing a feast, a covenant to convene.

Unleavened bread broken, shared with care,
Symbol of body, love's weight to bear,
In this simple act, a sacred embrace,
A covenant of redemption, a boundless grace.

The cup passed, filled with wine's hue,
Shared among friends, a bond renewed,
The blood of the covenant, Jesus proclaimed,
A promise sealed, in His name acclaimed.

A moment of communion, unity profound,
In bread and wine, a connection unbound,
The Last Supper's legacy, a covenant's start,
A call to remember, a devotion's heart.

Meditation: As Jesus institutes the Eucharist, this poem encourages us to consider the sacredness of this act of remembrance and the covenant of love and sacrifice it represents. This passage underscores the enduring significance of communion in the Christian tradition, a ritual that invites believers to partake in the spiritual fellowship and connection with Christ. Reflect on the depth of Jesus' relationship with His followers and the symbolism of the bread and wine.

Servant's Love – *John 13:1-20*

In an upper room's hush, a scene unveiled,
Jesus rose from the table, love detailed,
A basin, a towel, humility's plea,
A lesson of service, an act so free.

Disciples reclined, eyes met in surprise,
As Jesus knelt, to their shock and their sighs,
He washed their feet tenderly, a task so low,
A servant's heart, His love to bestow.

Peter resisted, humility's weight,
But Jesus insisted, love's message innate,
A lesson profound, as feet were made clean,
A symbol of grace, a bond unforeseen.

"Unless I wash you," Jesus spoke low,
A cleansing of heart, love's quiet flow.
He set the pattern, showed us the way—
A servant's heart in full display.

Meditation: The act of washing feet symbolizes Jesus' willingness to serve and sacrifice for the sake of His disciples, and it serves as a powerful reminder of the selfless love that should characterize the lives of His followers. Reflect on Jesus' servant-hearted example, which teaches us the importance of putting others before ourselves and embracing a humble attitude.

Shadows of Betrayal – Matthew 26:21-25

Around a table gathered, shadows deep,
A heaviness in the air, secrets to keep,
Jesus spoke of betrayal, a truth unveiled,
A friend's treacherous path, a bond derailed.

The disciples leaned in, uncertain and low,
"Is it I, Lord?"—they needed to know.
One by one, their hearts did sway,
As Jesus spoke of a traitor's way.

Judas, his question a mask for deceit,
Jesus saw through, his intentions complete,
"A friend who dips," the sign he'd see,
A prophecy foretold, a truth to be.

Judas' heart veiled in darkness and greed,
A plot set in motion, a soul's desperate need,
In his choice to betray, a story unfolds,
A lesson in loyalty, a tale retold.

Meditation: Judas' actions serve as a stark reminder of the consequences of choosing personal gain over faithfulness, and his question highlights the inner struggle between deceit and authenticity. Reflect on the complexities of loyalty and betrayal, which showcase how even in the closest circles, deception can lurk.

The Weight of Denial – John 13:31-38

In the Upper Room's sacred space, hearts weighed down,
Jesus spoke of departure, a foreboding sound,
A new commandment given, love to define,
Among His disciples, a legacy to shine.

Peter, impulsive and bold, questioned aloud,
"Where are you going?" his concern unbowed,
Jesus' response veiled in mystery and pain,
A path of suffering, redemption's gain.

Peter's confidence soared, loyalty declared,
Even if all falter, he'd stand prepared,
But Jesus saw beyond the words he'd speak,
A night of denial awaited, truth to seek.

"Before the rooster crows," Jesus declared,
Thrice denial would come, truth laid bare,
Peter protested, disbelief in his eyes,
Yet a lesson in humility, in failure's guise.

Meditation: Peter's fervent declaration of loyalty contrasts starkly with his subsequent denial, serving as a reminder of the fragility of our commitments. The passage calls us to examine our own hearts, to humbly acknowledge our weaknesses, and to seek a genuine and enduring faith that remains steadfast in times of trial. Contemplate the complexities of human nature, our propensity for overconfidence, and the vulnerability of faith under pressure.

The Cup of the New Covenant – *Luke 22:17-20*

Around the table, disciples gathered near,
A sacred moment, Christ's presence clear,
With bread in hand, Jesus spoke with grace,
"This is my body, given for you," he'd trace.

A symbol of His sacrifice, a covenant new,
Binding hearts to grace, love shining through,
The broken bread, a unity proclaimed,
In Christ's name, disciples forever named.

Likewise, the cup, He raised with care,
"This is my blood," a promise to bear,
The cup of the covenant, forgiveness divine,
A symbol of redemption, in every sip, a sign.

His body broken, His blood outpoured,
A covenant sealed, a future assured,
A bond of love, a gift of salvation,
In every meal, a divine invitation.

Meditation: The passage emphasizes the profound connection between Christ's sacrifice and our communion with Him. The act of partaking in the bread and cup becomes a tangible representation of Christ's eternal mission of redemption and His invitation to partake in the grace He offers Reflect on the deep symbolism of the bread and the cup, representing Christ's body and blood, as well as the new covenant forged through His sacrifice.

A Promise of Comfort – *John 14:1- John 17:26*

In the upper room, a tender scene,
Jesus' words flowed like a peaceful stream,
"Do not let your hearts be troubled," He began,
A promise of comfort, a steadfast plan.

"I am the way, the truth, and the life," He proclaimed,
A guide through darkness, a path unblamed,
Through Him, the Father's love is known,
A unity of hearts, a truth sown.

The Comforter came, God's holy breath,
To guide through life, to comfort in death.
In truth He speaks, in hearts He stays,
A boundless Spirit through all our days.

"I will not leave you as orphans," He assured,
A promise of love, eternally secured,
His words a testament of love's divine,
In His name, a power to intertwine.

As the hour drew near, Jesus' prayer arose,
A plea for unity, as love interflows,
For all believers, a bond so true,
Reflecting the love, the Father knew.

Meditation: This poem encapsulates the themes of comfort, guidance, unity, and the indwelling presence of the Holy Spirit. These chapters emphasize the intimate relationship believers share with Christ, the promise of the Holy Spirit's presence, and the unbreakable bond of love between Jesus and His followers. It also underscores the importance of unity among believers and the significance of Christ's intercessory prayer. As we journey through these verses, we are reminded of the eternal mission of Christ to draw us closer to the heart of God, offering us comfort, guidance, and the assurance of His unending love. Reflect on Jesus' role as the way, the truth, and the life, and find comfort and guidance in His promises.

Gethsemane's Agony – Matthew 26:30-46

In the shadow of Gethsemane's night,
A heavy heart, a soul in plight,
Jesus and His disciples found their place,
An atmosphere heavy with sorrow's grace.

Breaking bread, sharing a last meal,
A moment's communion, deep and real,
Judas' departure, betrayal's path,
Darkness descending, casting its wrath.

To the garden, Jesus led the way,
A place of prayer, where he'd stay,
Sorrow and anguish, He began to bear,
A weight of humanity, a burden to share.

"Let this cup pass," He earnestly prayed,
Yet surrendered to the Father's plan laid,
His disciples nearby, but they slept on,
Unaware of the battle He faced till dawn.

Three times He prayed, in sweat and pain,
Submission and struggle, a spiritual strain,
"Your will be done," He finally said,
A surrender profound, in darkness He tread.

An angel's presence, a source of might,
Strengthened the Savior through the night,
Gethsemane's garden, a place of surrender,
Where God's will met humanity's contender.

Meditation: The garden scene is a poignant reminder of Jesus' humanity and His obedience to the divine plan, despite the intense anguish He experiences. This poem draws attention to the disciples' slumber and Jesus' solitary struggle, highlighting the contrast between His inner turmoil and their lack of awareness. Through this moment, we witness the depth of Jesus' love for humanity and His willingness to endure suffering for the sake of redemption. Reflect on the depth of Jesus' emotions as He faces the reality of His crucifixion and willingly surrenders to God's will.

BETRAYED WITH A KISS – *MATTHEW 26:47-56*

Amidst the shadows of Gethsemane's vale,
Judas approached, his heart set to betray,
With a kiss of deceit, a facade so frail,
The plan set in motion; night turned to day.

A cohort of soldiers, swords gleaming bright,
With lanterns and torches, they came prepared,
The Teacher they sought, the scene set alight,
A friend's betrayal, a moment declared.

"Whom do you seek?" Jesus calmly inquired,
A question that held more than met the eye,
"I am he," He affirmed, courage inspired,
Amidst the betrayal, he'd not deny.

Peter's swift defense, a sword unsheathed,
A futile attempt, for the path was clear,
This was the plan, the cup he'd received,
To fulfill the purpose, dispel all fear.

In surrender, Jesus' hands were bound tight,
His followers scattered, fear held sway,
The garden's silence witnessed the plight,
Of the Savior betrayed in the darkest of days.

Meditation: This poem captures the tension and drama of that moment, as the betrayer approaches with a seemingly innocent gesture, yet harboring deceit. The portrayal of Peter's impulsive defense and Jesus' calm response emphasizes His commitment to the divine plan, even in the face of betrayal and imminent arrest. Pay attention to the juxtaposition of loyalty and treachery and contemplate the complexities of human choices and the contrasting responses of the disciples. This pivotal moment marks the beginning of Jesus' journey to the cross and underscores the price of redemption through His sacrifice.

The High Priests Inquiry – *John 18:2*

In the garden's shadows, a tense scene unfolds,
Soldiers and officials, a story to be told,
Betrayal's embrace, a kiss so profound,
Judas' act of deception, truth unbound.

Bound and led, the Teacher they sought,
Jesus, the Messiah, His fate was caught,
Before Annas, the high priest, He was brought,
An inquiry begun; a moment fraught.

Questioned of disciples and teachings he'd shared,
Jesus stood firm, His response declared,
"Ask those who've heard," He replied with poise,
The truth he'd unveil, no cunning ploys.

A slap to the face, a rebuke unearned,
Jesus' dignity upheld, though insult burned,
An example of composure, strength untamed,
Amidst the injustice, His character proclaimed.

Before Annas and Caiaphas, the trial ensued,
Religious leaders sought to subdue,
Yet the Lamb of God, His purpose intact,
A journey to the cross, salvation's pact.

Meditation: This poem highlights Jesus' calm demeanor and unwavering truthfulness in the face of false accusations and insults. The exchange underscores Jesus' commitment to His mission and His willingness to endure suffering for the sake of humanity's redemption. Reflect on the strength of Jesus' character and the contrast between His integrity and the unjust treatment He received, a poignant reminder of the sacrifice Jesus willingly made on behalf of all.

In the Courtyard's Chill – *John 18:12-23*

In the chill of the courtyard, a fire's glow,
Peter stood, uncertain, emotions in tow,
Jesus, now bound, inside the high priest's hall,
Denial's shadow loomed, fate's silent call.

Around the fire, the servants did gather,
Accusing glances, suspicion's tether,
"Are you one of His disciples?" they inquired,
Peter's voice quivered; fear transpired.

With three denials, the cock's crow a refrain,
Peter's heart sank, guilt's heavy chain,
Yet Jesus' gaze met his, understanding deep,
Love's compassion, forgiveness to keep.

Before the high priest, the Savior stood tall,
Questioned of teachings that challenged them all.
Silent He stood as the falsehoods flew,
A witness of truth, steadfast and true.

Struck by a guard, a blow undeserved,
Jesus' response measured, grace preserved,
In the courtyard's chill, a glimpse of God's plan,
Redemption's story, the hope of all man.

Meditation: This poem captures Peter's struggle with fear and his subsequent denials, juxtaposed with Jesus' unwavering integrity and composed response to false accusations. It is a reminder of Jesus' deep understanding of our weaknesses and His willingness to extend grace even in our moments of failure. Reflect on the themes of human frailty, the contrast between human weakness and Christ's strength, and the powerful message of forgiveness and redemption that emerge from these events.

The Mocking Trial – Matthew 26:57-68

In the dimly lit chamber, a trial begun,
Accusations hurled, the night's darkness spun,
Jesus, the accused, before the council stood,
A mock trial of injustice, deceit pursued.

False witnesses brought forth, their stories entwined,
Twisting the truth, darkness enshrined,
Accusations flowed, yet Jesus remained still,
Silent in the face of lies, according to His will.

"Tell us, are you the Christ?" they demanded,
Jesus' reply, His identity candid,
"You have said so," a truth unveiled,
Messiah's presence, though mocked and assailed.

Blindfolded, spat upon, the mocking began,
Insults and taunts, humanity's sin,
The very Creator, the King of all lands,
Subjected to cruelty, by human hands.

Amidst the mockery, Jesus stood strong,
Silent dignity in the face of wrong,
The Suffering Servant, bearing the shame,
Redemption's plan, through His holy name.

Meditation: Consider the immense injustice and cruelty that Jesus endured for our sake, His steadfastness in the face of mockery, and the incredible depth of His love for humanity. The contrast between the Son of God's humility and the world's arrogance is evident, highlighting the power of Christ's sacrifice amid human folly.

Denial and Redemption – *Matthew 26:58-75*

In the courtyard's glow, a fire's warmth near,
Peter lingered, his heart wrought with fear,
A bystander's glance, a question of doubt,
"Are you with Jesus?" they queried, no shout.

Three times the question echoed, clear and strong,
Three times denial followed, Peter's heart wrong,
Fearful and trembling, his loyalty crumbled,
As Jesus' prediction, the rooster's crow humbled.

Yet in that moment, a Savior's grace,
Jesus' gaze met Peter's, a steadfast embrace,
The weight of his failure, Peter could bear,
For in Jesus' eyes, forgiveness was there.

The dawn's light broke, a new day begun,
Peter wept bitterly, redemption's sun,
From denial's depths, a lesson profound,
Forgiveness and grace in Christ's love abound.

Meditation: This story serves as a reminder of the human struggle with faith and the immeasurable grace of Christ, which brings restoration even in the face of our failures. It also highlights the transformative power of Christ's forgiveness and redemption, as demonstrated through Jesus' compassionate gaze that met Peter's eyes. Reflect on Peter's moment of weakness, his denial of Jesus, and the subsequent flood of remorse.

The Verdict of Truth – Luke 22:66-71

In the shadow of night, a somber scene set,
The council convened, hearts with intent met,
Jesus before them, questioned and tried,
Accusations hurled; truth's veil denied.

"Are you the Christ?" they cried with disdain,
Their hearts set to judge, their verdict plain.
Jesus replied with a voice calm and bold—
"The Son of Man, as the prophets foretold."

Their verdict proclaimed, "You are the Christ, it's true,"
Yet their hearts remained hardened, their vision askew,
Mocking and scoffing, they questioned His claim,
In their hearts, truth's light struggled to flame.

The trial continued, a verdict proclaimed,
Blasphemy charged, truth and falsehood framed,
Amid the darkness, Jesus stood firm,
The embodiment of truth, His purpose confirmed.

Meditation: This poem invites us to reflect on the irony of the situation, where the truth of Jesus' identity as the Christ clashes with the hardened hearts of those who accuse Him of blasphemy. Despite their verdict, Jesus remains steadfast in His truth, demonstrating His unwavering commitment to His divine purpose. Examine your own heart and consider how you respond to the truth that Jesus embodies, and whether your life aligns with His teachings.

The Weight of Regret – *Matthew 27:3-10*

In the aftermath of a fateful deed,
Judas, consumed by remorse's seed,
Betrayal's price, his heart now knows,
Thirty pieces of silver, a heavy throe.

Seeking solace, redemption's path to find,
He returned the silver, guilt intertwined,
"I have sinned," he confessed with despair,
An acknowledgment heavy in the air.

The chief priests and elders, their hearts cold,
Refused the returned price, the story told,
A field of blood, the purchase made,
A tragic tale of a soul betrayed.

Judas' despair led to a tragic end,
A rope, a tree, a life to expend,
In death's embrace, he found no release,
A soul entangled in guilt's caprice.

Meditation: Judas' story serves as a reminder of the importance of seeking redemption and forgiveness, and the tragic outcome of allowing guilt to consume one's heart. This passage prompts us to consider how we handle our mistakes and the need for healing through God's grace and mercy. Reflect on the consequences of betraying trust, the heavy burden of regret, and the destructive power of unchecked guilt.

Before the Judgement Seat – Luke 23:1-7

In the early light of a fateful morn,
A scene of accusation, hearts forlorn,
Jesus before Pilate, a ruler's domain,
A trial that would shape history's chain.

Accusations hurled, voices raised,
A charge of sedition, a claim to be phased,
"Are you the king?" Pilate inquired,
As the crowd's accusations grew higher.

Jesus stood in silence, calm and serene,
A mystery in His eyes, a truth to glean,
He neither affirmed nor denied the charge,
A response that left the crowd at large.

Pilate, perplexed, sought for a way,
To navigate this trial, to find light of day,
He sent Jesus to Herod, a different scene,
An attempt to divert the turmoil's sheen.

Meditation: This poem draws attention to the tensions of the trial, the conflicting accusations, and Jesus' enigmatic response. Pilate's struggle to understand Jesus' identity and navigate the complex situation reflects the challenge of discerning truth in a world of manipulation and power dynamics. Consider the nature of truth, the weight of accusation, and the role of human authority in the face of divine purpose.

Herod's Curiosity – *Luke 23:6-12*

From Pilate's realm to Herod's domain,
Jesus stood before him, not in disdain,
Herod's curiosity piqued that day,
He sought a sign, a miracle's display.

Yet Jesus, silent, held no defense,
No miracle performed, no recompense,
Herod's hopes dashed, his questions grew,
Seeking answers from this enigmatic Jew.

Accusations and taunts from chief priests arose,
Their voices fierce, their intentions exposed,
Jesus remained unyielding, a steadfast grace,
Amid the turmoil, in this sacred space.

Herod's mockery and robes so fine,
Sent Jesus back to Pilate's line,
A pawn in their schemes, a pawn in the game,
Jesus' purpose beyond human acclaim.

Meditation: This poem highlights Herod's intrigue and curiosity about Jesus, as well as Jesus' steadfastness during accusations and mockery. This encounter reflects the complexity of human motivations and the contrast between earthly power and the divine purpose that Jesus embodies. Consider the significance of Jesus' silence, the nature of true authority, and the tension between the temporal and the eternal.

Mockery and Scorn – *Matthew 27:27-30*

In suffering's shadow, the scene grew grim,
Soldiers encircled, hearts dark and dim.
A robe of purple, a thorn-wrought crown,
They mocked the King, then struck Him down.

The King of Kings, in humble state,
Enduring humiliation, bearing the weight,
They bowed in jest, they laughed in glee,
Unknowing that they mocked Divinity.

A reed they placed, a scepter of jest,
They knelt before Him, in their own conquest,
Yet little did they comprehend,
The King they scorned, the Savior's end.

With thorns that pierced, with robe that clung,
A regal image in anguish wrung,
They taunted and jeered, a spectacle they made,
Unaware of the price he'd soon have paid.

Meditation: This poem highlights the irony of their actions, as they unwittingly mocked the true King of Kings. Reflect on the contrast between human perception and divine reality, the willingness of Christ to endure humiliation for the sake of humanity, and the profound message of humility and sacrifice that His suffering conveys.

The Journey to Calvary – *John 19:16-17*

Amidst the crowds, a hush and cry,
He walked beneath a darkened sky.
To Calvary's hill, through scorn and chill,
He bore the cross—God's holy will.

The weight of the cross upon His back,
A symbol of suffering, a love that won't crack,
Step by step, the journey commenced,
A path of sacrifice, a fate advanced.

Soldiers and onlookers, a scene of despair,
Yet in His eyes, a burden he'd share,
The Savior's footsteps marked the way,
To redemption's cross, to night's darkest day.

Through streets and alleys, to the hill's height,
He carried His cross, a beacon of light,
For in that journey, a world would see,
The price of salvation, the gift of mercy.

Meditation: Ponder the weight of the cross that symbolizes the burden of our sins, the sacrifice made for humanity's redemption, and the depth of Jesus' love for us. The journey becomes a poignant symbol of His unwavering commitment to fulfill His mission of salvation, guiding our hearts toward the ultimate act of selflessness.

A Mother's Sorrow – *John 19:18-27*

Upon the hill of sorrow and pain,
A cross was raised, a life to sustain,
Jesus hung between earth and sky,
A sacrifice given, for sins to deny.

Soldiers cast lots for His garments, cold,
As Mary stood by, a story of old,
A mother's heart pierced by grief and love,
Witnessing the sacrifice from above.

Beside her, the disciple whom He loved,
Jesus entrusted her, a bond unremoved,
"Mother, behold your son," He said,
A new family formed, in love's thread.

From that hour, the disciple cared,
As a mother's anguish, Jesus shared,
A son's embrace, a mother's tears,
A scene of love amidst sorrows and fears.

Meditation: This poignant scene serves as a reminder of the cost of redemption and the intimate relationships formed through the bond of faith. Contemplate the depth of Mary's sorrow and love, the significance of the disciple's role in caring for her, and the interconnectedness of the human family within the context of Christ's ultimate sacrifice.

Darkness and Victory – Matthew 27:45-50

Upon the hill, a darkness fell,
As midday sun concealed its swell,
Jesus, the Son, bore agony's weight,
Upon the cross, love and fate.

From noon till dusk, the heavens wept,
A veil of sorrow across Earth crept.
"*Eli, Eli, lema sabachthàni?*"—His plea,
Forsaken, yet forging our path to be free.

A sponge with sour wine, they pressed,
To His lips, offered a taste distressed,
His thirst met, His purpose clear,
The final moments drawing near.

With a loud cry, He breathed His last,
The ground quaked, a world aghast,
The temple veil tore, from top to bottom,
A new covenant's birth, sin's ransom.

Meditation: Amidst the darkness, this poem also hints at the ultimate victory that would emerge from this sacrifice—the tearing of the temple veil symbolizing access to God and the birth of a new covenant. Contemplate of the darkness that shrouded the land during those hours, signifying the weight of sin and separation from God that Jesus endured on behalf of humanity.

The Veil of Mystery – *Luke 23:45-49*

Amidst the crucifixion's solemn hour,
A veil of mystery descends with power,
The sun's light obscured by darkened skies,
Creation itself, in mourning, cries.

At noon, a shroud of darkness spreads,
Around the cross where hope now treads,
A trembling earth, a cosmic sign,
In this moment, divine and earthly intertwine.

Within the temple, the veil was torn,
From top to bottom, a message born,
Access granted to the Holy place,
Through Christ's sacrifice, God's grace.

Soldiers and bystanders witness the scene,
The Lamb of God, sin's chasm in between,
Some struck with awe, a centurion's voice,
"Truly this was the Son of God," his choice.

Meditation: Ponder the significance of these cosmic and symbolic phenomena—a powerful representation of the divine mystery of Jesus' sacrifice and the newfound access to God's presence through the rending of the veil. Reflect on the centurion's acknowledgment of Jesus' identity, pointing to the impact of Christ's crucifixion on even those who were witnesses to the crucible of redemption.

The Silent Tomb – Mark 15:42-46

As evening shadows lengthen, a somber hush,
The lifeless body of Christ, the sacrificial brush,
Joseph of Arimathea, a man of noble creed,
Requests the body, fulfilling a sacred need.

A new tomb hewn from rock, a resting place,
Where the Savior's body finds a solemn grace,
Linen cloth, a gesture of honor and care,
The silent tomb receives Him, a moment to bear.

The stone rolled against the entrance, sealed tight,
A sentinel of death, shrouded in night,
Yet within its depths, a divine plan unfolds,
Redemption's story in the silence it holds.

The body of Jesus, in the tomb's embrace,
A moment of transition, God's saving grace,
For in the silence, hope's seed was sown,
Awaiting the dawn, the empty tomb to be shown.

Meditation: The silence of the tomb serves as a bridge between the crucifixion and the triumphant resurrection, emphasizing the transformative power of Christ's sacrifice. Contemplate the stillness and reverence of this act, the symbolism of the tomb as a seed of hope for resurrection, and the significance of Jesus' temporary resting place.

THE EMPTY TOMB – *LUKE 24:1-11*

In early morning's gentle light, a group arrives,
Women with spices, their hearts' love alive,
At Jesus' tomb, they find a startling scene,
The stone rolled away, an unexpected glean.

Entering the tomb, perplexed hearts in awe,
Angelic figures appear, a message to draw,
"Why seek the living among the dead?" they say,
"He is not here; risen as He did convey."

Remembrance of Jesus' words comes to mind,
The promise of resurrection, a truth defined,
The women return to the disciples' side,
Sharing the news of the tomb open wide.

Yet disbelief taints their words, a skeptic's thought,
The resurrection's mystery, yet to be sought,
The empty tomb stands as a silent proof,
Of Christ's victory, truth's unending roof.

Meditation: This poem underscores the central role of the empty tomb in proclaiming the triumph of life over death and the fulfillment of Jesus' promise. Reflect on the awe-inspiring moment of discovering the tomb's emptiness, the women's role as bearers of the good news, and the challenge of grasping the profound reality of Christ's resurrection.

Dawn of Resurrection – *John 20:1-10*

In the predawn hush, Mary Magdalene arrives,
At the tomb of Jesus, her heart heavy with cries,
The stone removed, an empty chamber she sees,
Panic sets in, a mystery to appease.

Running to Peter and John, she conveys the tale,
"The Lord is taken!" her voice filled with travail,
Peter and John hasten to the tomb's embrace,
Discovering linen cloths, a strange empty space.

John believes, though the full truth eludes,
A resurrected Christ, a notion to include,
Yet Mary lingers, tears clouding her sight,
Two angels appear, in robes of pure light.

"Why do you weep?" they inquire with care,
Mary's heart's ache, her sorrow to share,
Then a voice behind her, a gardener she perceives,
Until "Mary," He speaks, and her heart believes.

"Rabboni," she calls, recognizing His tone,
Jesus, her teacher, her Lord fully known,
Resurrection's dawn, a new day begins,
The victory over death, a triumph that wins.

Meditation: This poem emphasizes the intimate and personal nature of Jesus' resurrection appearances, as well as the transformative power of encountering the risen Christ. Reflect on the mixture of emotions that filled Mary's heart, the gradual dawning of faith in the resurrection, and the profound encounter that solidified her belief.

Risen Hope – *John 20:11-18*

At the tomb's entrance, Mary Magdalene stands,
Her heart still heavy, her tears wet the sands,
Inside she peers, two angels in white,
"Why do you weep?" they inquire in the morning light.

"They've taken my Lord," her voice quivers with sorrow,
A stolen body, a hope for tomorrow,
A voice behind her, tender and kind,
"Whom are you seeking?" she's asked to define.

Thinking he's the gardener, she seeks the way,
"Sir, if you've moved Him, please, I pray,
Tell me where you've laid Him, I'll take Him away,"
A devotion unswayed, her love on display.

"Mary," He calls, with a voice known so well,
The scales fall from her eyes, the story they tell,
"Rabboni!" she exclaims, her heart now ablaze,
In Jesus' resurrection, her hope finds its rays.

"Do not cling to me," He gently imparts,
A mission awaits, a message to start,
"Go to my brothers, proclaim the good news,
I ascend to my Father, a journey to choose."

Mary obeys, her heart set aflame,
A witness of resurrection's fame,
In encountering Jesus, her life is reborn,
A risen hope, a new dawn's morn.

Meditation: This poem emphasizes the personal and intimate nature of Jesus' appearances after His resurrection, as well as the call to share the good news of His victory over death. Mary's experience exemplifies the hope and transformation that the resurrection brings to all believers.

Reflect on the depth of Mary's grief, her journey from sorrow to astonishment, and her transformative encounter with the resurrected Christ.

The Web of Deceit – Matthew 28:11-15

A tale of deceit, a bribe well plied,
Among the guards, the truth denied.
They fled to the city, their faces pale,
Of angels and emptiness, they dared not tell.

Chief priests and elders, a plan they wove,
To silence the truth, the story to remove,
A sum of silver, a bribe to sway,
"Say His disciples came and stole Him away."

The guards agreed, their pockets lined,
With ill-gotten gain, their conscience maligned,
A fabricated tale, deception in the air,
To suppress the truth, a false narrative to declare.

But rumors spread, truth's whispers grew,
Beyond the guards' control, the story flew,
The empty tomb's message, a truth unbound,
Jesus had risen, victory resound.

Meditation: This poem reveals the contrast between human efforts to suppress the truth and the unstoppable power of the resurrection message that ultimately spread far and wide. The poem serves as a reminder of the enduring impact of Christ's resurrection and how attempts to conceal the truth are ultimately futile in the face of God's divine plan. Reflect on the lengths to which some were willing to go to deny the resurrection's reality.

The Road to Emmaus – *Luke 24:13-35*

On a dusty road, two hearts weighed down,
Conversing in sorrow, faces cast in a frown,
Unbeknownst to them, a traveler drew near,
Jesus Himself, their hearts to steer.

He walked beside them, their story to glean,
Their downcast faces, their hopes unseen,
"Tell me," He inquired, His words a balm,
Their tale of the Crucified, their hearts in a calm.

As they walked and talked, the miles flew by,
He opened the Scriptures, their souls to apply,
From Moses to prophets, He unveiled the way,
A narrative of redemption, from darkness to day.

At Emmaus' inn, the hour grew late,
They urged Him to stay, to share in their fate,
He took the bread, blessed, and broke it apart,
In that sacred act, recognition sparked in their heart.

Their eyes were opened, the veil cast aside,
The stranger before them was the risen Christ,
In joy and amazement, they marveled anew,
The resurrected Savior, their faith renewed.

Meditation: The unveiling of Jesus in the breaking of bread serves as a reminder of His abiding presence and the transformative power of encountering the risen Christ. Just as the disciples' hearts burned within them, this poem encourages us to seek Christ's presence in our own journey of faith. Reflect on how Jesus walks alongside us in our moments of confusion and disillusionment, guiding us through the Scriptures to a deeper understanding of God's redemptive plan.

Thomas Believes – *John 20:26-31*

In an upper room, a gathering of friends,
Joyful hearts and hopeful amends,
But Thomas, absent, missed the sight,
The risen Jesus, shining in light.

"Unless I see His hands and side,
My doubts won't cease, my faith won't ride,"
Thomas declared, his heart sincere,
A faith struggle he held so dear.

A week went by, and gathered again,
The disciples present, hearts filled with gain,
Jesus appeared, His scars displayed,
A living proof, the price He paid.

"Touch and see, my wounded hands,
Believe, Thomas, in my divine plans,"
Tears flowed, doubt's chains released,
Thomas proclaimed; his faith increased.

"Blessed are those who don't see but believe,"
Jesus' words a balm, hearts to relieve,
Thomas found the truth he'd sought,
In Christ's resurrection, his faith was caught.

Meditation: Thomas' honest doubts and subsequent transformation serve as a reminder that Jesus welcomes our questions and meets us in our uncertainties. Through Thomas' experience, we are encouraged to embrace a faith that seeks understanding and find solace in the words of Jesus, affirming the blessedness of believing without seeing. Contemplate the nature of faith and doubt. Just as Thomas found his belief deepened through his encounter with the risen Christ, this poem encourages us to anchor our faith in the reality of Jesus' resurrection and the transforming power of His presence in our lives.

A Miraculous Catch – *John 21:1-25*

Beside the sea, disciples gathered 'round,
Peter, Thomas, others renowned,
A night of toil, a fruitless catch,
Till Jesus appeared, their hope to match.

"Cast your nets on the other side,"
His voice carried on the morning tide,
A miraculous catch, abundance anew,
Fishermen astounded; their doubts withdrew.

Peter, the impulsive, plunged to the shore,
To meet his Lord, His heart to explore,
Jesus cooked breakfast, a meal of grace,
A reminder of love, in every embrace.

Threefold questions, Peter restored,
Forgiveness extended, His purpose underscored,
"Feed my sheep," Jesus' command,
A role of leadership, in God's hand.

John, the beloved, by Peter's side,
Two disciples in whom love did abide,
A glimpse of futures, a race to the end,
Following Jesus, on Him to depend.

Meditation: The miraculous catch of fish symbolizes the abundance and blessings that come when we obey Christ's instructions, even when they seem unconventional. The breakfast scene serves as a poignant reminder of Jesus' intimate care and the nourishment He provides for both body and soul. The dialogue between Jesus and Peter highlights the process of restoration after Peter's denial and reinforces the importance of loving and serving others. The poem concludes by emphasizing the individual paths of Peter and John, illustrating the uniqueness of their callings and the commitment to follow Jesus. Contemplate the theme of restoration and purpose. Just as the disciples responded to Jesus' call, this poem encourages us to embrace our roles with purpose, to seek restoration in Christ, and to follow Him with unwavering love and dedication.

The Great Commission – *Matthew 28:16-20*

Upon a mountain, disciples convened,
Resurrected Christ, their hearts believed,
Though some doubted, uncertainties sown,
Jesus' presence reassured; His authority known.

"All authority in heaven and on earth is mine,"
His words like stars in the night did shine,
A mission proclaimed, a purpose divine,
"Go and make disciples of all nations, for this is my design."

Baptizing in the name of the Father, Son,
And Holy Spirit, the triune One,
Teaching obedience to every command,
Guided by His presence, in every land.

Lo, He promised to be with them always,
Till the end of days, in myriad ways,
A promise of comfort, a beacon of light,
Empowering disciples, in faith to take flight.

Meditation:. The mountain setting in this passage serves as a symbolic backdrop, reminiscent of the divine encounters that have taken place on elevated terrain throughout Scripture. The phrase "All authority in heaven and on earth is mine" highlights Jesus' sovereignty over all realms, both earthly and spiritual. His command to make disciples reflects the heart of His mission, urging believers to extend His teachings and invite others into the fold. The act of baptizing and teaching underscores the holistic nature of discipleship, encompassing both initiation and ongoing growth in faith. The poem culminates with Jesus' assurance of His abiding presence, offering comfort and empowerment as believers embark on the journey of fulfilling the Great Commission. Just as the disciples were called to go, baptize, and teach, this poem encourages readers to embrace their role in spreading the message of Christ, confident in His enduring companionship. Contemplate the significance of Christ's authority and the mandate He gave to His disciples before ascending into heaven.

Ascension's Blessing – *Luke 24:50-53*

On Olivet's mount, a moment sublime,
Jesus lifted His hands, marking the time,
His farewell spoken, His blessing outpoured,
A sacred transition, an eternal reward.

As they beheld, His form taken away,
He ascended to heaven, the culmination of His stay,
Yet hearts were not heavy, nor burdened by loss,
For His promise endured, the comfort of the cross.

A mix of awe and joy, disciples gazed,
Upon the Savior, who their sins erased,
Heaven and earth united in that gaze,
As Christ's presence lingered, an eternal blaze.

With hearts full of worship, they returned to the city,
Their purpose emboldened, their souls full of glee,
In the temple, they praised, in unity they prayed,
The Ascension's blessing, in their hearts displayed.

Meditation:. The imagery of Jesus lifting His hands in blessing underscores His role as the ultimate High Priest and mediator between heaven and earth. The disciples' mixed emotions of awe and joy reflect the complex blend of reverence and elation that accompanies divine encounters. The assurance that Christ's promise endures, even in His physical absence, serves as a source of comfort and inspiration for believers. The scene also illustrates the unity between heaven and earth, as the eternal and the temporal intersect in this moment of ascension. Contemplate the significance of this event, marking the completion of Christ's earthly ministry and His return to the Father As the disciples returned to the city to praise and pray, reflect on your own response to Christ's ascension, seeking to live out the blessing and purpose it imparts.

Appendix

Penning the Gospels: Exploring the Lives of the Gospel Writers

The Gospel narratives, which illuminate the life, teachings, and legacy of Jesus Christ, hold an unparalleled significance in the realm of spiritual literature. Behind these timeless texts lie the unique perspectives and backgrounds of their authors—Matthew, Mark, Luke, and John.

In this exploration, we embark on a journey through the biographies of these Gospel writers, uncovering the individual lives that shaped their perspectives and influenced the words they penned. From tax collectors to physicians, each author brings their distinct experiences, insights, and encounters with Christ into the narratives they crafted.

Join us in delving into the lives of these inspired individuals, discovering how their diverse journeys converged to create a harmonious and multifaceted portrait of Jesus' life and ministry. Through their lenses, we gain a deeper understanding of both the Gospel message and the devoted individuals who dedicated their lives to its preservation.

Matthew: The Tax Collector Turned Disciple

Matthew, also known as Levi, is one of the twelve apostles of Jesus Christ and the author of the Gospel of Matthew, a cornerstone of the New Testament.

In his pre-discipleship life, Matthew was a tax collector in Capernaum, a profession that often-garnered distrust and resentment from the Jewish community due to its association with collaboration with Roman authorities. However, it was during his daily routine that Jesus, the great teacher, and healer, called Matthew to follow Him. This pivotal moment altered the trajectory of Matthew's life forever. His transformation from a tax collector to a devoted disciple reflects the redemptive power of Christ's message.

After accepting Jesus' call, Matthew left his tax booth and became a devoted follower, committing himself to the teachings and ministry of Jesus. As one of the chosen twelve apostles, Matthew had a front-row seat to witness miracles, parables, and profound conversations with the Messiah. He experienced the transformative power of Christ's message firsthand and absorbed the teachings that would later shape his Gospel account.

Matthew's Gospel is distinctive in several ways. It begins with a genealogy tracing Jesus' lineage back to Abraham, underscoring His identity as the fulfillment of Old Testament prophecies. This emphasis on connecting Jesus to Jewish heritage was likely influenced by Matthew's background and his desire to demonstrate to his fellow Jews that Jesus was the long-awaited Messiah.

The Gospel of Matthew highlights Jesus' teachings, including the Sermon on the Mount, where He addresses topics such as humility, forgiveness, and love for enemies. This Gospel also contains unique parables and emphasizes Jesus' role as the fulfillment of Old Testament prophecies. Additionally, Matthew's Gospel places a significant emphasis on Jesus' authority and His commission to spread the Gospel message to all nations.

Traditionally, Matthew is believed to have composed his Gospel in the Aramaic language before it was later translated into Greek. While the exact timeline of its composition remains debated, its enduring significance is unquestionable.

Matthew's life journey from a tax collector to an apostle showcases the transformative impact of encountering Jesus Christ. His Gospel remains a valuable resource, offering a unique perspective on the life and teachings of the Savior, making Matthew a vital contributor to the rich tapestry of the New Testament.

Mark: The Swift Evangelist

Mark, often identified as John Mark, is recognized as one of the authors of the New Testament and the writer of the Gospel of Mark. His role in early Christianity and his contribution to the Scriptures provide a unique perspective on the life and teachings of Jesus Christ.

Although not one of the twelve apostles, Mark is believed to have been a close associate of both Peter and Paul, two prominent figures in the early Christian community. It is widely accepted that Mark's Gospel is influenced by the teachings and experiences he received from Peter, making it an account that carries the apostolic authority of an eyewitness.

Mark's Gospel is characterized by its succinct and fast-paced style. It reads like a narrative, presenting Jesus' actions and teachings with a sense of immediacy and energy. Mark's focus on action-driven scenes and concise descriptions reflects his intention to convey the transformative impact of Jesus' ministry on those who witnessed it.

One notable feature of Mark's Gospel is its emphasis on Jesus' miracles and healing acts. Through these accounts, Mark portrays Jesus as the compassionate and powerful healer who reaches out to those in need, both physically and spiritually. Mark's portrayal of Jesus' miracles resonates with his own understanding of Jesus' mission as one of restoration and redemption.

Mark's Gospel also portrays the human side of Jesus, emphasizing His emotions and reactions in various situations. This portrayal adds depth to Jesus' character and allows readers to connect with His humanity, ultimately contributing to a holistic understanding of His nature as both divine and human.

While the Gospel of Mark is often described as the shortest and most direct of the four Gospels, its brevity does not diminish its significance. Mark's writing style captures the urgency and impact of Jesus' message, compelling readers to consider their response to the good news of salvation.

Mark's association with Peter and his commitment to conveying the Gospel message in a vivid and impactful way make his Gospel an invaluable contribution to the New Testament. His role as an evangelist, faithfully transmitting the teachings and actions of Jesus, inspires believers to engage with the message of Christ's redemption and salvation.

Luke: The Compassionate Historian

Luke, the author of the Gospel of Luke and the Acts of the Apostles, is a figure whose contributions to the New Testament provide valuable insights into the life and ministry of Jesus Christ and the early Christian community.

Traditionally known as Luke the Evangelist, he was likely a Gentile and a physician by profession. His Gospel and the book of Acts reveal his meticulous attention to detail and historical accuracy, reflecting his desire to present an orderly and comprehensive account of the events he witnessed and researched.

Luke's Gospel stands out for its emphasis on compassion, social justice, and the inclusivity of Jesus' ministry. He often portrays Jesus' interactions with marginalized individuals, women, and those considered outsiders in society. Through these accounts, Luke highlights the transformative power of Jesus' love and the message of salvation for all.

One of the distinctive features of Luke's Gospel is his thorough investigation and careful documentation of events. His prologue states his intention to provide an accurate and well-ordered account based on eyewitness testimonies. This commitment to historical accuracy lends credibility to the Gospel's narrative and underscores Luke's dedication to preserving the truth of Jesus' life and teachings.

In addition to his Gospel, Luke also authored the Acts of the Apostles, which serves as a continuation of the Gospel narrative. This book chronicles the growth of the early Christian church and the spread of the Gospel message. Luke's depiction of the apostles' struggles, successes, and challenges provides a comprehensive view of the early Christian movement.

Luke's contributions to the New Testament reflect his deep empathy for humanity and his desire to present a holistic portrait of Jesus Christ. His emphasis on Jesus' teachings about compassion, forgiveness, and reconciliation resonates with his own values and underscores the transformative power of the Gospel message.

As a Gentile writer, Luke's Gospel reflects a universal perspective, emphasizing the gospel's relevance and applicability to people of all backgrounds. His meticulous research, compassionate approach, and commitment to historical accuracy make his writings essential resources for understanding the life of Jesus and the growth of the early Christian community.

John: The Spiritual Theologian

John, known as the author of the Gospel of John, the three Johannine Epistles, and the Book of Revelation, presents a unique and profound perspective on the life, teachings, and divinity of Jesus Christ. Often referred to as the "Beloved Disciple," John's writings are characterized by their deep spiritual insights and theological depth.

John's Gospel stands apart from the Synoptic Gospels (Matthew, Mark, and Luke) due to its distinct style and content. While the Synoptics focus on narrative and events, John's Gospel delves into the spiritual and theological significance of Jesus' life and ministry. John's emphasis on Jesus as the eternal Word and the incarnate God highlights his profound understanding of Christ's divinity.

In his Gospel, John employs symbolism and metaphor to convey deeper truths about Jesus' identity and mission. Using "I AM" statements, miracles, and discourses, he unveils the spiritual reality behind the physical world. The famous prologue of his Gospel eloquently presents Jesus as the Word made flesh, emphasizing His role in creation and salvation.

John's Gospel also highlights the themes of love, light, truth, and eternal life. The "new commandment" to love one another and the allegory of the Good Shepherd illustrate his focus on the transformative power of Christ's love and the intimate relationship between Jesus and His followers.

The Johannine Epistles and the Book of Revelation further showcase John's deep spiritual insights and his emphasis on love, obedience, and the victory of Christ. His letters encourage believers to remain faithful, practice genuine love, and reject false teachings. The Book of Revelation unveils apocalyptic visions and offers hope amid trials, revealing Christ's ultimate triumph over evil.

John's writings reflect his profound relationship with Jesus as a close disciple and his role as a witness to Christ's life, death, and resurrection. His theological depth, spiritual insight, and emphasis on love and divine truth continue to inspire and guide believers on their spiritual journeys. Through John's lens, readers are invited to explore the mysteries of the divine and encounter the transformative power of Christ's eternal message.

A Chronological Journey Through the Life of Christ

1. Annunciation and Birth (c. 6 BC - c. 4 BC):
   - Angel Gabriel appears to Mary, announcing her pregnancy with Jesus.
   - Mary and Joseph travel to Bethlehem for the census.
   - Jesus is born in Bethlehem, laid in a manger.

2. Visit of the Magi and Flight to Egypt (c. 4 BC - c. 6 AD):
   - Wise men from the East follow a star to find Jesus and offer gifts.
   - An angel warns Joseph in a dream to flee to Egypt to escape Herod's massacre of infants.

3. Return to Nazareth and Growing Years (c. 6 AD - c. 26 AD):
   - Mary, Joseph, and Jesus' return to Nazareth.
   - Little is recorded about Jesus' upbringing and early life.

4. Baptism and Early Ministry (c. 26 AD - c. 30 AD):
   - Jesus is baptized by John the Baptist in the Jordan River.
   - Jesus begins His public ministry, performing miracles and preaching about the Kingdom of God.

5. Calling of Disciples and Teachings (c. 30 AD - c. 33 AD):

- Jesus calls His first disciples, including Peter, Andrew, James, and John.
- Jesus delivers the Sermon on the Mount, teaching about ethics, love, and the Kingdom of God.
- Parables like the Good Samaritan and the Prodigal Son are shared to convey spiritual truths.

6. Transfiguration and Final Ministry (c. 33 AD):
   - Jesus is transfigured on a mountain, revealing His divine glory.
   - He continues to heal, teach, and confront religious leaders' hypocrisy.

7. Final Week and Crucifixion (c. 33 AD):
   - Jesus enters Jerusalem triumphantly on Palm Sunday.
   - He cleanses the temple and engages in intense theological debates.
   - The Last Supper takes place, where Jesus institutes the Eucharist.
   - Jesus is arrested, tried, and sentenced to death by crucifixion.
   - He is crucified on Golgotha, where He dies and is buried in a tomb.

8. Resurrection (c. 33 AD):
    - On the third day, Jesus rises from the dead, conquering death.
    - He appears to His disciples and others, confirming His resurrection.
    - The Great Commission is given to the disciples to preach the Gospel to all nations.

9. Ascension and Early Church (c. 33 AD - c. 100 AD):
    - After forty days, Jesus ascends into heaven in the presence of His disciples.
    - The Holy Spirit descends on the disciples during Pentecost, empowering them.
    - The early Church spreads the message of Christ's redemption, facing challenges and persecution.

Miraculous Moments and Where to Find Them

List of Christ's Miracles and Scripture References*

Water into Wine - John 2:1-11

Healing the Nobleman's Son - John 4:46-54

Healing the Paralytic - Matthew 9:1-8, Mark 2:1-12, Luke 5:17-26

Calming the Storm - Matthew 8:23-27, Mark 4:35-41, Luke 8:22-25

Healing the Demon-Possessed Man - Matthew 8:28-34, Mark 5:1-20, Luke 8:26-39

Healing the Woman with the Issue of Blood - Matthew 9:20-22, Mark 5:25-34, Luke 8:43-48

Raising Jairus' Daughter - Matthew 9:18-19, 23-26, Mark 5:22-24, 35-43, Luke 8:41-42, 49-56

Healing the Blind Men - Matthew 9:27-31

Feeding the Five Thousand - Matthew 14:13-21, Mark 6:30-44, Luke 9:10-17, John 6:1-14

Walking on Water - Matthew 14:22-33, Mark 6:45-52, John 6:15-21

Healing the Canaanite Woman's Daughter - Matthew 15:21-28, Mark 7:24-30

Feeding the Four Thousand - Matthew 15:32-39, Mark 8:1-10

Healing the Blind Man at Bethsaida - Mark 8:22-26

Healing the Deaf and Mute Man - Mark 7:31-37

Healing the Blind Man in Jerusalem - John 9:1-41

Healing the Man with a Withered Hand - Matthew 12:9-14, Mark 3:1-6, Luke 6:6-11

Healing the Demon-Possessed Boy - Matthew 17:14-21, Mark 9:14-29, Luke 9:37-43

Catching a Fish with a Coin in Its Mouth - Matthew 17:24-27

Healing the Blind and Mute Demon-Possessed Man - Matthew 12:22-23, Luke 11:14

Healing the Woman with a Spirit of Infirmity - Luke 13:10-17

Healing the Man with Dropsy - Luke 14:1-6

Healing the Ten Lepers - Luke 17:11-19

Raising Lazarus - John 11:1-44

Healing the Blind Man near Jericho - Matthew 20:29-34, Mark 10:46-52, Luke 18:35-43

Withering the Fig Tree - Matthew 21:18-22, Mark 11:12-14, 20-24

Restoring the Severed Ear - Luke 22:47-53

The Miraculous Catch of Fish - John 21:1-14

*This list covers the major miracles performed by Jesus as recorded in the Gospels, along with the corresponding Scripture references.

The miracles showcase Jesus' divine power, compassion, and the fulfillment of prophecies, revealing His role as the Messiah.

www.ingramcontent.com/pod-product-compliance
Lightning Source LLC
Chambersburg PA
CBHW020244010526
44107CB00002B/90